Make,
Mend,
Bake,
Save &
Shine!

Make, Mend, Bake, Save & Shine!

With tips from Oxfam's Green Granny
Barbara Walmsley

Written by Jo Godfrey Wood

spruce

An Hachette UK Company

First published in Great Britain in 2010 by
Spruce, a division of Octopus Publishing Group Ltd
Endeavour House, 189 Shaftesbury Avenue, London, WC2H 8JY
www.octopusbooks.co.uk

Copyright © Octopus Publishing Group Ltd 2010

Produced by **Bookworx**
Editor: Jo Godfrey Wood, Designer: Peggy Sadler
Jacket design and book development: Eoghan O'Brien
Illustrator: Harriet Russell

978-1-84601-367-6

A CIP catalogue record of this book is available from the British Library.

Printed and bound in China

10 9 8 7 6 5 4 3 2 1

All royalties from this book go to Oxfam.

© **Mixed Sources**
Product group from well-managed
forests, controlled sources and
recycled wood or fiber
www.fsc.org Cert no. SGS-COC-003548
© 1996 Forest Stewardship Council
FSC

CONTENTS

6
Introduction

8
chapter 1
Handy at home

58
chapter 2
Yummy food for less

110
chapter 3
Thrifty fun for everyone

INTRODUCTION

Barbara Walmsley, 'Oxfam's Green Granny', has been an ardent supporter of Oxfam for several decades. Because of her passion for the charity's work she raises thousands of pounds every year with a sponsored fast; her unique, innovative way of demonstrating that there are so many starving people around the world who need help. She has also turned her energy to setting up Oxfam's specialist bridal shops, which raise substantial sums for the charity's important development work.

Barbara's support for Oxfam is very much part of her approach to everyday life. She's a dynamic lady with an infectious enthusiasm for making a difference and for sharing what she can with others. As well as raising money, Barbara, like Oxfam itself, is committed to promoting sustainable living. Part of that is about reusing, recycling and cutting energy use, where possible. A less wasteful, more efficient, 'greener', lifestyle is a how we can all play our part in building a better future. It is Barbara's hope that in passing on some of her thrifty how-to tips in this book, she can contribute to the efforts we can all make. Now let's hear from Barbara herself:

"When an opportunity arose to become Oxfam's 'Green Granny' I didn't hesitate for a moment. All my life I've struggled to suppress my enthusiasm and I've failed miserably! I wanted to put my energy to good use and attract as much attention to Oxfam's cause as possible. Since I was sixteen I have been in the street rattling a collecting tin – now, in my early seventies, I'm still at it. For 24 years, every November, I've been sitting outside our local supermarket with a label round my neck reading 'Do not feed – I'm fasting for Oxfam'.

Every year I raise thousands of pounds for Oxfam's work fighting poverty and suffering. On top of that I started the Oxfam bridal business from our back bedroom and now we have twelve Oxfam bridal boutiques around the UK, with a thirteenth opening soon.

Why do I do all this? Because I am so lucky. I don't have to scavenge on a rubbish tip for food, work in a sweat shop and I don't have to watch my children die of sickness because there is no clean water. There are so many people for whom real hardship is an everyday reality and I want to make a difference to them. The effects of climate change are adding to their problems and our wasteful lifestyle is making things worse. We can all do our bit and I hope that this book will help you do your bit too. We can do so much, not just by giving money, which is terribly important, but by reusing, recycling, being thrifty and being green in our everyday lives."

In this little book, Barbara passes on a lifetime of valuable thrifty skills on how to be a green domestic goddess. With energy-saving tips, recycling know-how and a dose of wholesome common sense, you can learn, for example, how to use up leftovers, make do and mend, declutter and recycle, shop for seasonal bargains and clean like a dream for a fraction of the cost. If you want to do more for less, if you're branching out on your own, or if you just want to learn how to cut your waste, these household hints and tips will revolutionize the way you live.

You can find out more about Oxfam's work, how to volunteer, donate or get involved at www.oxfam.org.uk. All Oxfam's work needs funding and Oxfam's network of staff and volunteers work tirelessly to raise money to overcome poverty and suffering.

~ chapter 1 ~

Handy at home

Your home is your sanctuary and there are masses of easy things you can do to make it a truly special place. There's no need to spend a lot – the thriftier you can be, the better. Try these hints and tips to keep your space clean, your possessions in order, your clothes looking better for longer and your budget under control.

HOME CARE **KITS**

To take proper care of your home, whether big or small, you need to assemble some basic toolkits. The kits listed here will see you through the ordinary things you need to attend to. Just add or subtract as required. Charity shops, such as Oxfam, and car boot sales are great places to stock up on second-hand items.

Cleaning clobber

- ✔ Cloths and dusters (old cut-up T-shirts are good)
- ✔ Brush & dustpan
- ✔ Broom
- ✔ Hoover
- ✔ Scouring pads
- ✔ Bucket
- ✔ Floor mop
- ✔ Lemon juice
- ✔ Old toothbrushes
- ✔ Bicarbonate of soda
- ✔ Vinegar

DIY repairs

- ✔ Screwdrivers
- ✔ Spanners
- ✔ Pliers
- ✔ Hammers
- ✔ Scrapers
- ✔ Chisels
- ✔ Saws
- ✔ Stanley knife
- ✔ Tape measure
- ✔ Spirit level

Sewing kit

- ✔ Sewing machine
- ✔ Scissors
- ✔ Pins
- ✔ Tape measure
- ✔ Thread

Gardening tools

- ✔ Spade
- ✔ Fork
- ✔ Rake
- ✔ Hoe
- ✔ Watering can

- ✔ Secateurs
- ✔ Trowel
- ✔ Bucket
- ✔ Wheelbarrow
- ✔ Daisy grubber

First-aid kit

- ✔ Plasters
- ✔ Surgical tape
- ✔ Scissors
- ✔ Bandages
- ✔ Paracetamol
- ✔ Aspirin

- ✔ Antiseptic
  cream & wipes
- ✔ Triangular
  bandage
- ✔ Thermometer
- ✔ Safety pins

- ✔ Tweezers
- ✔ Cotton wool
- ✔ Wound
  dressing pad

GREEN CARE & CLEANING

A clean home is important, but it's also important not to get too obsessive about a bit of a mess. After all, having a super-clean home isn't the be-all and end-all. It's best to do what you can, when you can, and to leave bigger jobs for when you have more time. This section gives you hints and tips on how to clean and care for the basic rooms in your home.

There are cleaning agents you can buy for every possible cleaning chore, but many of them are unnecessary, quite apart from being expensive and very often bad for the environment. They introduce damaging chemicals into the home and eventually into the waste-water system. Try making your own cleaning agents from a few basic store cupboard ingredients, and see how effective (and green) they are. They'll save you a fortune too.

DON'T FORGET!
Have a shoes-off policy in your home. That way less outside dirt will be tracked in.

KITCHEN

The hub of the happy home – this area is normally the main target for cleaning and keeping dirt-free. Happily, there are plenty of cheap, easy and green ways to keep everything under control. A lot of households use the kitchen to eat in as well as to cook in – this saves a lot of trouble carrying food into another room and keeping that area clean, but it puts extra wear and tear on the kitchen. Don't forget to keep all receipts and guarantees of appliances safely.

Kettle What would your home be without a kettle? Just think of all those wonderful cups of tea! However, it's easy to let limescale build up. To descale fill it with half water and half vinegar and leave it to sit overnight before emptying, wiping out, refilling with water, reboiling, emptying, filling and reboiling again. By this time you'll be in serious need of a good cuppa!

Oven Use a mixture of elbow grease and natural ingredients to make an impact on your oven (clean it regularly to prevent heavy build-up). Try mixing a thick paste of mildly abrasive cleaner by adding a few drops of water to bicarbonate of soda. Paste this over the inside of the oven, leave it overnight and then scrub vigorously with water, using a scouring pad.

Hob The thrills and spills of hob-dom! The best plan is to have a cloth handy and to keep using it. That way you don't get a nasty build-up of gunk that's almost impossible to remove later. Use warm water and a little washing-up liquid for light stains and a mix of bicarbonate of soda and water for heavier marks.

Worktops It's important to keep all surfaces
as clean as possible, so mop up spills as you
go along. But worktops really need a proper
wipe-down after every use and a little washing-
up liquid in warm water is fine for this. To make an
all-purpose cleaner mix bicarbonate of soda with lemon juice. If
you have tiles and grouting, you'll need to scrub between the tiles
with a solution of one part bleach to four parts water. Old toothbrushes are ideal for getting into all the dirt-holding crevices.

Dishwasher It is not necessary to rinse plates before putting them
in but do scrape off food scraps. Clear out the filter regularly and
occasionally run a short cycle while the machine is empty, with a
cup of white vinegar to help get rid of limescale and slimy grease
build-up. To save energy, only run the machine with a full load.

GREEN GRANNY SAYS...

"If you only use a half
a dishwasher tablet per wash
your dishes will still be
sparkling clean."

Floor As a quick clean-up – keep a broom handy and give the kitchen a once-over every day (if you have the time). Then plan to have a go-over with a mop weekly. The best non-toxic floor cleaner is quarter of a cup of mild washing-up liquid added to a bucket of warm water.

Fridge It's a great idea to clean the fridge out weekly, wiping the inside with a mix of two teaspoons of bicarbonate of soda per litre of warm water. To eliminate smells just leave an open container of bicarbonate of soda at the back. After you've had a go at the rubber seal, where germs can accumulate if you're not careful, do the same for the outside.

Sink If you have time it's a good plan to wipe the sink down every time you use it and disinfect it with a capful of bleach and warm water. Have a go at the overflow with an old toothbrush. Get rid of stains with a little vinegar and try a bicarbonate of soda paste on any stains in stainless-steel sinks. Lemon juice will help shift limescale. Try not to let bits of food and old tea leaves clog up the plughole. You can buy special sink strainers to avoid this, but if, despite your best efforts, you do have to unblock, try the traditional plunger first. Seal it to make it airtight and then press the plunger quickly up and down. This should shift things. To clean or clear drains, pour half a cup of bicarbonate of soda down and chase it with a cup of hot vinegar.

BATHROOM

Bathrooms are well used these days, although this was not always the case. Once upon a time bathrooms tended to be chilly and unwelcoming places, where hot water was limited and showers practically non-existent. These days people treat them as sanctuaries and use them for private spa sessions (see pages 134–9) so extended use means extra cleaning.

Loo Hands up anyone who likes this job! But it's got to be done and daily cleaning is a must. If you are trying to limit flushing (every other pee) to save water you may find the loo is more prone to staining. If you want to limit the water the loo uses, put a brick in the cistern. To shift stains, put soda crystals in overnight and flush in the morning. Cola down the loo has the same de-staining effect, but five teaspoons of bicarbonate of soda mixed with boiling water and left overnight should shift things.

Shower A shower uses less water than a bath, but you could still remind home-sharers not use it for hours on end. However a clogged shower head will limit how much water you receive, so this needs regular descaling. Do this by removing the shower head and soaking it in vinegar overnight. Give it a really good scrub and rinse it off thoroughly before attaching it again. Nasty mould appearing in shower sealant can be a problem. Household bleach may help get rid of small patches, but avoid it starting by keeping the bathroom well aired – either by opening windows or using an extractor fan – and wipe down everything after use.

Water, water everywhere

Water is a precious commodity and it should be treated with the respect it deserves. It's up to us to save it rather than squandering it and there are plenty of easy ways to do this all around the house.

→ Don't let the tap run while you are cleaning your teeth (you can waste gallons this way – if a family of four don't clean their teeth under running water for a year, the water they save would fill an Olympic-sized swimming pool). Mixer taps also waste water. You could catch water as it is warming up and use it for houseplants.

→ Take showers rather than baths, but be aware that power showers can use lots more water than normal showers.

→ It's fine to drink tap water. No need to pay extra to get it in plastic bottles (which you'll have to recycle anyway).

→ Collect rainwater in a water butt and use the water on your garden and for watering houseplants. If you're really dedicated you could investigate having the butt plumbed directly into your washing machine or loo – a relatively cheap and easy process.

→ Make sure all water-using appliances are only used fully loaded. Otherwise water is wasted.

Bath A quick go-round the bath with a soft cloth and mild cleaner will keep nasty rings at bay, but a really bad case will benefit from being filled with warm water plus two scoops of biological washing powder and left overnight. Don't scrub an enamel bath as you'll scratch it, but you can treat stains with a paste of bicarbonate of soda and water. For cast-iron baths, get rid of limescale with a half vinegar, half water solution.

LAUNDRY AREA

Washing, drying and ironing are time-consuming activities and they use up a lot of energy. This section gives you some easy hints and tips on how to care for your most important appliances and keep them clean and also how to make the business of keeping clothes clean a little easier – and greener.

Washing machine Your machine is important to you! So be kind to it and it'll be kind to you. Be sure to unclog the filter – all kinds of stuff gets caught in there. Wipe over the detergent drawer with a soft cloth (old cut-up T-shirts are good) and if you need to attack nooks and crannies, reach for an old toothbrush.

It's a good idea to run your washing machine empty periodically on a hot wash with a little vinegar – to stop it cooking up nasty smells, limescale and mildew. Avoid using water and electricity by limiting the number of washes you do. Wear clothes more than once and refresh them by hanging them outside for a while. When you fill the machine, check that it's a full load: small loads waste energy.

🐞 Think about halving the amount of detergent you put into the machine. It's in the interests of the manufacturer to sell as much detergent as possible, so instructions usually tell you to use more than you need – much more. Your clothes will come out just as clean if you use less. Experiment to see how little you can get away with.

🐞 When it comes to keeping clothes nice and clean, spare a thought for your energy consumption. Setting your washing machine to 60 degrees is usually unnecessary – or usually only justified for towels, sheets, handkerchiefs and stained items. For things that have only been worn once or are not too dirty, use a low temperature (40 or even 30 degrees). You'll find that things come out just as well and you'll be saving energy. For bedding, if you have allergies or an infestation use the 60 degree setting as lower temperatures will not have any effect on bed bugs or dust-mites. Duvets usually need dry-cleaning, but some are washable – check the label.

Dump the dryer? It sounds drastic, but why not dump the dryer? Or, at least, fail to buy a new one if yours happens to die a death? Unless you have no access to outdoor space, have you considered getting a clothesline and pegs? It's possible to dry clothes out of doors most of the year, even in colder climates, and you only need a small area to set up a fold-up whirligig dryer. It's good for your environmental footprint and good for your washing as the sun zaps bugs and germs. Plus your clothes will benefit from the fresh air – they'll smell great! Letting clothes have a good blow means they'll need less ironing. Again – less electricity – a greener you!

Iron Ironing can seem like drudgery, but some people like it. If you want to limit the amount you do, shake your clothes out briskly when removing from the washing machine or dryer, hang them on hangers on the line to dry before folding them. You'll find that a lot of items don't really need ironing. Also, if clothes aren't on view, such as the trusty T-shirt you wear under a sweater, maybe it doesn't need ironing at all.

Dry-cleaning for dummies

Is it really necessary to have everything with a 'dry-clean only' label dry-cleaned? Could it be hand washed (in cold water) instead? Many items are OK to be hand washed. However, trial and error can be expensive when dealing with dry-clean-only clothes, so try this only if you are confident of success. There are some fabrics that will only be suitable for dry-cleaning, in any circumstances. If in doubt, find out more before putting prize dry-cleanables in the washing machine. Some people only ever buy items that can be washed in a machine so it pays to look at the care labels before you buy.

Green Granny's ironing tips

- When the washing is dry gently pull each item into shape and fold it neatly or hang it on a hanger. This will minimize creases and make ironing easier.
- Some fabrics need dampening before ironing. Sprinkle the item with warm water, roll it up tightly and leave for an hour.
- To iron a shirt, start with the collar, then iron the sleeves and cuffs. Lastly tackle the front and back.
- To iron a round tablecloth, it's best to start in the middle and work towards the perimeter.
- Hang trousers, jackets and dresses in a steamy bathroom to get rid of wrinkles. This is great when you are travelling.

Keep your iron clean

Limescale can seriously clog your iron's reservoir or soleplate and it's a good idea to keep both as free of it as you can.

→ To get rid of limescale fill the reservoir with a mixture of water and vinegar and leave it there for a couple of hours. Then tip it out and rinse with fresh water.

→ Refresh the soleplate by giving it a good polish with a cloth when the iron is cold (an old cut-up T-shirt is fine). If your iron has sticky marks on it, dampen your cloth lightly and heat the iron up before polishing. If the marks won't just wipe off, you could try using bicarbonate of soda or toothpaste.

BEDROOM

These havens of intimacy and cosiness are probably lowest on the lists of priorities for most home-cleaners. You sleep in them, keep your clothes in them and maybe watch a bit of TV or read in them, but they don't usually get a lot of muddy traffic. They just need to be kept aired and clutter-free. Most of the time, it's quite enough to just keep bedrooms dust-free and hoovered once a week. However, bedrooms can also harbour pests – moths and dust-mites being the most common.

Moths Moths love it if your clothes (especially woollen ones) are left unattended and tightly packed for long periods. If you've got a lot of clothes squashed together in the dark, warm wardrobe, you might be receiving an unwelcome moth-attack – so be careful! If you put your favourite woolly sweater at the bottom of a full drawer for the summer, especially if you forgot to wash it first, you will probably find it full of holes the next time you want to wear it. But luckily you can take action!

Things you can do:
🦋 Wash your woollies before putting them in moth-proof bags.
🦋 Shake your clothes out regularly (moths hate light and movement) and keep storage spaces clean. Vacuum carpets regularly, especially in tight corners, under beds and behind furniture. Empty the hoover straight away to get rid of eggs, larvae or moths.

DID YOU KNOW?
The higher the duvet tog rating the warmer the duvet will be. A low rating is 4.5 and a high rating is 13.5.

Pillow & bed care

✔ Fluff pillows daily to keep them plump and cosy.

✔ Use good-quality pillow and mattress protectors – they will prolong the life of your bedding. Wash them occasionally.

✔ When you get out of bed, strip back the duvet to allow the bed to air. Moisture accumulates overnight. It will help if you open the bedroom windows as well.

✔ Change your sheets once a week. If you want to cut down on washing use two flat sheets and move the top sheet to the bottom. Just wash the bottom sheet each week. Regular washing helps to cut down dust and kills dust-mites.

✔ Hang your bedding in the sun to kill dust-mites.

🖖 Use mothballs, though they will only be a partial solution alongside cleaning. The balls produce vapours that will kill insects, but they work best in an airtight container.

🖖 Cedar chests and cedar balls may help repel moths for a while, but they lose their effectiveness over time.

Dust-mites These are a pesky problem if anyone in the household suffers from asthma allergies and you will need to be extra vigilant in the dust-busting department. Apart from indulging in regular dusting – around once a week – you'll need to wash all the pillows on a high temperature annually and vacuum mattresses. Mites that have got into small items can be killed by putting them in the freezer (in a plastic bag).

WHOLE-HOUSE CLEANING

If, like most of us, you lead a busy life, most likely the rest of your home just needs to be kept clutter-free, reasonably tidy and cleaned through once a week-ish. Sudden spills, of course, need to be sorted out when they happen. De-cluttering (see also page 28) will help your home 'seem' clean and make it easier to keep clean anyway.

More than ever, our homes are sanctuaries from our busy lives and the hectic world, so we need to feel cosy and relaxed there. Here are a few hints and tips on how to achieve simple green cleaning:

Windows Most of the time it's better to get a proper window-cleaner to clean the outsides of windows – especially if they are high up. Don't take risks on ladders. However, inside you can probably take care of most of the window-cleaning. Half-water, half-vinegar solution is great for all glass, including mirrors. Use newspaper on windows to get a really great shine. You can also use warm water with a dash of washing-up liquid.

Curtains Eliminate nasty smells from curtains by spraying them with a solution of two parts water and one part vinegar. If they suffer fading, after washing re-hang them the other way round, so that the previous outer edges now hang on the inside, where they catch the light. This way they'll fade evenly and last longer.

Venetian or slatted blinds Wear an old cotton glove moistened in a solution of equal parts of white distilled vinegar and hot tap water. Slide your fingers across both sides of each slat and wash off the glove periodically in clean water.

Radiators Hang a damp cloth or some sheets of damp newspaper behind the radiator. Then blow on the radiator with a hairdryer so that you force hidden dirt and dust onto the damp cloth or newspaper.

DID YOU KNOW?
Where furniture has dented a carpet, fill the dent with an ice cube and when it has melted brush it out.

Carpets To remove spots and stains mix a solution of one part distilled white vinegar to five parts water and put it into a spray bottle. Fill up a second bottle with one part white, non-sudsy ammonia and five parts water. Saturate the stain with vinegar solution, wait a few minutes, then blot it with a clean cloth. Spray the area with ammonia solution, wait and then blot again. Repeat until the stain is gone. If you want to get rid of smells in the carpet sprinkle it with plenty of

Green Granny's dust-busting tips

- Wash your dusters in vinegar to cut down the amount of lint that they produce.
- Use anti-static dusters on electronic equipment to reduce the amount of dusting you have to do in the first place.
- Hoover all the carpets at least once a week to remove the dust trapped in them as well as ordinary fluff.
- Slightly damp dusters help do a more thorough job of picking up dust from furniture and all polished surfaces.

bicarbonate of soda and vacuum up after about 15 minutes. If you want to bring an old rug back to life, brush it with a clean broom dipped in a solution of 225ml (one cup) of distilled white vinegar in four litres (one gallon) of water. There's no need to rinse afterwards.

TRY THIS

If your time is limited and your house is dirty just decide to spend 10, 30 or 60 minutes at a time.

Spring cleaning

Once a year it's a good idea to put aside a few days and clean your home from top to bottom. This will help you to keep on top of your clutter and maintain order in your life. Here is a checklist of tasks you might not ordinarily get around to during the rest of the year.

✔ Put away seasonal clothes (use vacuum-pack bags for moth protection and space saving).

✔ Check and clean your appliances (hoover behind the fridge, clean the dishwasher and the washing machine).

✔ Declutter (get rid of things you don't use – see page 28).

✔ Clean and tidy garages, patios and potting sheds.

✔ Clean and wash windows, curtains and blinds.

✔ Check over your bedding to see if anything needs replacing. Turn mattresses and wash mattress protectors.

PETS

Pets are great companions, but they need quite a bit of care and attention when it comes to keeping the home clean and odour-free. Pay special attention to kitchen areas.

Smells Rinse the cleaned cat litter tray and then pour about 12ml (half fl oz) of full-strength white distilled vinegar into the tray. Let it stand for about 20 minutes, then rinse with cold water. Dogs love to roll around, but if you notice a bad smell afterwards, add vinegar to its bath. When you wash your dog's blanket add 110ml (half cup) of white distilled vinegar to the rinse cycle. If your cat pees on washable material, mix 110ml (half cup) of white distilled vinegar and wash it as normal. To get rid of the smell from floors, carpets, rugs or upholstery, use vinegar to deodorize and stop the animal doing it again. On floors use equal parts of vinegar and warm water to mop the area, but test a small spot first. Use the vinegar undiluted on carpets, rugs or upholstery after blotting with a rag. Reapply vinegar and allow to air-dry.

Cages Mix a solution of one part white distilled vinegar to two parts water to clean your bird and hamster cages or rabbit hutch. After wiping with the vinegar solution wipe again with clean water. Vinegar is very effective for removing bird droppings.

Grooming Bicarbonate of soda works well as a dry shampoo and it also acts as a deodorant. Rub over your cat or dog's teeth for an answer to pet bad breath. To deter ticks and fleas add a teaspoon of apple cider vinegar to your pet's drinking water or fill a spray bottle with equal parts water and apple cider vinegar and spray the animal's coat before rubbing in well.

BE A DE-CLUTTERBUG

TIDY OR TIP?

You may already be a tidy soul, or perhaps a little more informal, but the time comes when you have to get your possessions in order – just to function properly and get on with your life. Here are some easy hints to follow, to help you on your way.

WHY YOU ACCUMULATE MORE 'STUFF'

You may go through phases of acquiring more things, while other times you are quite happy to prune down and live more simply. As your life changes, new possessions are acquired. A new partner means combining two people's possessions and perhaps an influx of joint ones, too. A precious baby means a long, ever-changing list of

Clutter corners

These corners seem to attract clutter, which seems to breed all by itself! Every home has odd places were stuff congregates: little piles of papers, pots of old pens, keys, reminders, hair grips – you name it! They seem to appear on mantelpieces, kitchen dressers and in all sorts of ledges and corners. After a while you get used to them – the best plan is to stop them happening in the first place or make regular times to weed them out.

essential equipment and cute little things; a new job means you to have to invest in some smart new clothes; a much-loved relative dies and leaves you some beautiful heirlooms. The list is endless. You just have to find a way of managing all the stuff in your life.

TAKE A LONG, HARD LOOK

If you wake up one day and find you can hardly move around your home for stuff – you need to take serious action. First, tidy up – it's hard to act if you can't see what's there because there's so much of it. Separate out things you no longer want. These may be unwanted presents or things you've stopped using because they're out of date or broken. Could you find another home for them? Don't be tempted just to throw things away – it's such a waste! Think 'recycle' and consider carefully whether you could find new homes for items. Would someone else be grateful to use your unwanted possessions? If you need to get rid of larger items, such as furniture, you will find it easy enough to swap, sell or give them away through recycling websites.

WHEN IN DOUBT, CHUCK IT OUT?

But, hold on! Not into your dustbin. Do you have a pile of things you don't want any more? Do you have broken things that you never seem to get around to mending? Do you have a stack of books that you know you'll never want to read again?

If someone else could use your cast-offs why not take them to a charity shop such as Oxfam? Someone poking casually around the shop might think that the vase Aunt Nelly gave you, but you've never liked, is just perfect for their mantelpiece (and it's a real bargain, too!) – and the charity gets their money. Everyone wins.

PUT IT AWAY, STRAIGHT AWAY!

Make a resolution to put everything away as you go along. For example, pick up and hang up all your clothes as you take them off and put everything for the wash in the laundry basket. Don't leave it until tomorrow. In the kitchen, clean down surfaces and put away ingredients when you've finished cooking.

'IT'LL COME IN HANDY ONE DAY'

Beware of hanging on to things 'just in case'. If you're not using it now, what would make you want to use it next week, next year, or in ten years' time? Could someone else be using it right now instead, if you could give it to them? It's taking up valuable space in your home. If you are lucky enough to have lots of storage cupboards, maybe an attic or even a cellar, beware of storing things that you don't really want any more. Storage space is a luxury, but just because you've got it, that's not a good enough reason to keep things if they're not being used.

> **DON'T FORGET!**
> Make use of old envelopes and scrap printout to make notebooks for shopping lists and reminders.

Paper trail

Have a rule about paper. Handle any piece of paper, such as a bill, coming into the house once only, so that it is dealt with straight away and then filed or recycled. That way papers don't gather and breed in piles and important letters get attended to straight away.

RETHINK YOUR SHOPPING HABITS!

We seem to love shopping these days. Many happy hours can be spent roaming the local shopping centre. There's so much to look at and it all looks so appealing – even if you don't actually buy. But the chances are you'll buy something just to make your trip seem worthwhile. Then, after the 'shopping buzz' has died down, you'll probably wonder why you bought it.

The sad thing is that we are all buying things we don't really want or need, or presents others don't want. This is creating too much stuff, too much manufacturing, too much energy use and a challenging predicament for our planet.

Why do we buy things? We just get caught up in a 'shopping moment' – maybe our companion talked us into buying, or we just felt like a bit of retail therapy. Think hard about only going shopping when you really need something. Let's face it, sprees aren't good for you, your pocket or the planet.

LOVE & CARE FOR YOUR CLOTHES

CLOTHES, CLOTHES, CLOTHES

We love 'em! Don't we? For some of us clothes are just a necessity, while for others they're nothing short of an obsession. Some people go into serious debt to fund their clothes habit, maxing out their credit cards in a bid to keep up with the regularly changing fashion scene. But this habit comes with a serious price tag – for ourselves and for the planet.

Your capsule wardrobe

If we buy a few, classic good-quality pieces and create a 'capsule wardrobe', which will stand the test of time, we'll be doing our purses and the planet a huge favour. Choose plain colours that go with each other and aim for variety by adding accessories (belt, scarf, jewellery, hair accessories, shoes and tights). These are the essentials you'll need in your wardrobe:

- ✔ One pair of jeans
- ✔ Two long-sleeved shirts
- ✔ Two T-shirts
- ✔ One cardigan
- ✔ Two sweaters

- ✔ Two pairs of trousers
- ✔ One jacket
- ✔ One skirt
- ✔ One dress
- ✔ One coat

Unfortunately cheap clothes mean cheap labour and in distant countries some workers being employed at exploitative rates and working in difficult conditions. The energy used, the materials needed, the water needed – all create an enormous drain on the planet's resources. Why not rein in your clothes-shopping habits and buy only the clothes you really need? Less consumption broadly means less use of energy and materials – and a greener way of life.

DON'T FORGET!
When you take clothes to the charity shop, such as Oxfam, make sure they are clean and in good condition,

RECYCLE YOUR CLOTHES

Clothes are the perfect thing to recycle. You may have fallen out of love with things you thought were great only a few months ago, or you may have lost or gained weight, so why not give someone else the chance to wear them? Sort out a sackful and take them down to your local charity shop, such as Oxfam. Or why not swap your clothes with a friend?

GREEN GRANNY SAYS...

"Clothes are the perfect thing to recycle. Sort out a sackful and take it to your local Oxfam shop."

HAND-ME-DOWNS ARE HIP!

When you were a kid and were perhaps given your big sister's old clothes to wear when she'd grown out of them, maybe you weren't so keen on this concept. But now you're a big girl – think again! Second-hand is 'vintage' and everyone's doing it. Great bargains are to be had at charity shops and vintage emporiums. Why not raid your mother's or grandmother's wardrobe for some unique pieces?

KIDDIE CLOTHES

Hand-me-downs make perfect sense. Babies cost a fortune, from the moment they're born, so why not pass around their cast-offs? Your little ones grow so quickly that their clothes hardly get any wear. Everyone will be saving their pennies and the clothes will be earning their keep by being worn by more than one baby. Why not hold a clothes-swap party for your group of mum-friends?

Have a 'swishing' party

→ Ask a bunch of friends round and get them to bring unwanted clothes, including at least one good-quality item, for a 'swishing' session. Spend a hilarious hour or two trying on each other's clothes and – if they suit – swap them for keeps. This is a great way to pass on wardrobe items you've fallen out of love with – and have fun at the same time. There are now organied events for swishing. Just look online for one in your area.

→ If your party is at home, support your favourite charity, such as Oxfam, by charging a small entry fee and/or pricing each item.

"So much clothing gets wasted —
it's our responsibility to get
as much use out of each item as
we possibly can."

Shoe and leather care

It's worth looking after your shoes and bags to give them a longer life. Classic leather bags stay in fashion for a long time, so it's worth the effort. Finding a good cobbler to repair well-loved shoes is better than chucking them out and buying new ones.

➜ To get rid of water marks on leather add one tablespoon of vinegar to 240ml (8fl oz) of water and apply with a soft cloth. Wipe and then polish in the normal way.

➜ Don't wear the same pair of shoes every day as the moisture needs time to evaporate. Rest them in between wearings.

➜ Stuff wet shoes with screwed-up balls of newspaper. Their shape will be maintained and they'll dry quickly. Don't dry them in front of a fire as the leather will dry up and crack.

➜ If your shoes get smelly sprinkle them inside with bicarbonate of soda. After a day or so shake them out and leave them to air.

MENDING IS A MUST!

Seriously! Fallen-off buttons, bust zips, split seams, little holes – you name it. These are all small jobs that you can easily tackle to extend the life of a beloved top or skirt. Forgotten how to do it? Or never learnt how to do it in the first place? Never fear – this book will give you some hints and tips and you'll never look back. Don't even think of throwing something out just because it's got something minor wrong with it.

Once you've got a decent capsule wardrobe (see page 32), you need to take care of it. It'll last longer that way. Be sure to mend something the moment it needs it. Don't let it become cluttering piles of mending, which you fully intend to do one day, but never quite get around to. It's never too late to learn a few key clothes-care tasks. For complicated jobs, you can ask your local dry-cleaner.

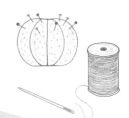

GREEN GRANNY SAYS...

"Mending is so important! If everybody mended their clothes instead of chucking them out and buying new, there'd be a lot less waste."

How to
Sew on a button

This is an easy job, which will extend the life of your favourite cardigan or skirt. If you've lost the button, go to a haberdasher's or search your local charity shops, such as Oxfam, for a replacement.

1 Take a needle and thread, thread the needle and knot the thread at one end.

2 Place the button on the front of the garment. From the back, prod the needle through one of the button holes, bring the thread to the front and reintroduce through another button hole to the back of the garment. If there are four button holes either stitch diagonally or in parallel.

3 Carry on until the button is held sturdily in place. If the button is on a coat or some other robust garment, do not pull it tightly to the garment but, after a few stitches, wind the remaining thread round and round to create a sturdy 'stalk'. This will stop the threads wearing through so quickly.

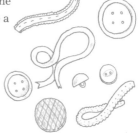

How to
Darn a jumper

**It's so annoying when your nicest jumper
gets a worn patch on one elbow or a tiny
moth hole. Here's how to darn all small
holes – extending your jumper's life.**

1 Use a child's ball to stretch the area to be
mended over. Thread your needle with
wool and begin to sew about 1.5cm (½in) to
the side and 1.5cm (½in) below the edge of the
hole. Start a running stitch, in and out, along
the length of the hole and then continue
across the hole and for 1.5cm (½in) on the
other side.

2 Sew another line of running stitches back
to the side you started on, right next to the
first line.

3 Continue sewing running stitches across
the hole. Be careful not to pull the wool
too tightly. Turn around and sew back again.
Repeat until the hole is covered and there is a
1.5cm (½in) border of stitches on each side.

4 Turn the jumper 90° and begin sewing a
line of running stitches across the stitches
already sewn. Repeat in the opposite direction
when you reach the end of your sewing.

5 Continue sewing back and forth, but now when you reach the hole, weave your wool through the stitches stretched across the hole. Take your needle over one stitch and under the next until you are past the hole, where you can continue a few running stitches. Then turn around and sew back again in the same fashion.

6 When the hole is completely covered, tie a knot and cut the wool. Turn the jumper right side out again and cut any wool ends that are protruding from the darned area. There – good as new!

How to
Sew on a patch

Patches have their fashion moments – you may want to make a feature of it and choose a fabric in contrasting colours. But make sure that it is more or less the same weight of material as the garment.

You Will Need

- Scrap of fabric for patch
- Needle & thread
- Pins

1 Cut the patch large enough to cover the hole or worn area, allowing enough material to fold the edges under.

2 Turn the edges under and pin the fabric over the worn area or hole.

3 Thread a needle and knot it at one end. Sew the patch onto the garment, around the turnings, as neatly as you can.

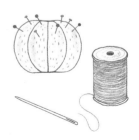

ALTERING & CUSTOMIZING

If you're good with a needle, have you ever thought of altering and customizing your clothes to extend their life? Most jobs are quite straightforward and you'll be proud of the results. Look at craft blogs for tutorials on tackling trickier projects or go to your local library for inspiration. Don't forget, if you're really stuck with a tricky task, dry-cleaners often do repairs and alterations.

ALTERING IDEAS

Shortening a hem will give an old, long dress a new lease of life.

Replacing a zip will allow you to wear that perfectly fitting pair of trousers once again.

Altering darts is easier than you think. If you've either gained or lost weight you can easily let darts out or take them in without losing the garment's basic style.

Mending tears can be done almost invisibly to extend the wear of a much-loved piece.

Taking in and letting out seams is a good way to make adjustments for figure changes as time goes by.

Adjusting waistbands, either in or out, is another way to get more life out of something you really like wearing.

When collars become frayed, unstitch them, turn them the other way round and restitch them to the shirt.

If you're good at dressmaking why not try converting an old adult coat into one for a child.

WHY NOT...
Collect old silk scarves from charity shops and turn them into funky cushion covers.

CUSTOMIZING IDEAS

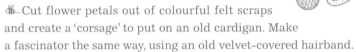

✂ Cut the legs off worn-out jeans to make shorts and fray the hems for a summer-holiday look. Use the leftover legs to make draught-excluders (stuff them with old socks and tights).

✂ Cut flower petals out of colourful felt scraps and create a 'corsage' to put on an old cardigan. Make a fascinator the same way, using an old velvet-covered hairband.

✂ Scared of 'embroidery'? Don't be. Try doing it 'freeform'. Choose bright embroidery silks, decorate an old pair of jeans – don't worry about using 'proper' stitches – make it up as you go along. Or try simple running stitch in bright lines around hems and cuffs .

✂ Change the colour of a shirt you would still love to wear but have grown bored with. Home-dyeing is easy – either hot-dye in the washing machine, or buy cold-water dyes.

✂ Change a garment by sewing on different buttons. New buttons can be pricey, so buy a charity-shop item and cut the buttons off.

Green Granny's customizing tips

✎ Use colourful braids to trim skirt hemlines to give a skirt an exotic 'gypsy' or 'peasant' feel.

✎ Unravel an old sweater and knit yourself something new, such as a cosy scarf or beanie.

✎ If you've an old polo-neck sweater, cut the bottom off just above the armpits to make a cute capelet.

✎ Keep your hands warm but active by cutting the fingers off old woollen gloves. Use the cut-off bits to make finger-puppets.

BECOME A HANDY DIY-ER

Things fail and cease to work on a daily basis around the home, but there's no need to call out an expensive repair person, unless it's something serious. Many small things are easy to mend yourself, if you know what you're doing. This is so much easier on your purse and you will gain great satisfaction from doing a good job.

Green Granny's DIY tips

- If you are worried about your tools getting a bit rusty – if you're not going to be using them for a while – coat metal bits with petroleum jelly before wrapping them up in brown paper.
- You can save leftover bits of putty to use again by wrapping them up in foil and keeping them in the fridge. They should be OK for about a year.
- Be sure to buy eco-friendly or natural paints.
- Before you go out and buy the latest flatpack have a look at the furniture you've already got. Could you re-cover an old sofa, paint a kitchen dresser or convert an old table into a low, sleek coffee table by shortening the legs?
- Take all your leftover equipment and refuse to your local recycling centre. They have dedicated bins for each type of waste, including your old lightbulbs, car batteries, unused paints and building rubble (if you've really had to knock everything down and start again).

How to change a
Lightbulb

Changing a lightbulb is easy once you know how – no need to ask for help.

DON'T FORGET

The next time you change your lightbulbs use long-life energy-saving versions.

1 Turn off the light fixture and allow the hot bulb to cool before touching it.

2 Grasp the bulb lightly but firmly and turn counterclockwise, until it is released from the socket. If it is a bayonet fitting use both hands and press upwards before turning.

3 Insert a replacement bulb lightly but firmly into the socket and turn it clockwise until it is snug. Turn the lamp or fixture back on and dispose of the used bulb at a recycling outlet.

How to change a
Fuse in a plug

These days plugs are made in one piece and changing a fuse is very straightforward.

1 On the plug side you will see a plastic panel. Using the two small slots remove each side and take out the fuse and carrier with a flat-head screwdriver.

2 Remove the fuse from its carrier, put in a new fuse of the same rating and push the fuse carrier back into the empty slots.

PAINTING & DECORATING

Whether you are trying to sell a property or you just want to give a room a facelift, a coat of paint is a great, cheap way to brighten up your surroundings. If you follow a few simple rules you'll make light work of the task.

🐝 Don't cut corners by buying cheap brushes, you'll find the hairs come off and ruin your work.

🐝 Don't buy more paint than you'll need and be sure to take any leftover paint to your local recycling centre. You will need about 5 litres (1⅛gal) of emulsion to cover 60sq m (65sq yd). Don't forget that if you are painting over a stridently patterned wallpaper or dark colours you will need to paint extra coats.

Sawing basics

Be very careful when using saws and power tools. Never use them if you are unsure how to and always keep children away. To start sawing place the blade on the edge of the wood. Dig in gently and draw back to make a small nick. Push the blade back and forth, keeping an angle of 45°. There are three main types:

➜ Hacksaw – can be fitted with interchangable blades and can cut metal and plastic pipes.
➜ Tenon saw – has fine teeth and can cut through wood, plastic and veneer.
➜ Power jigsaw – has a long, flat blade.

Make sure you cover furniture and floors with dust sheets in order to keep them free from paint splatters. Old sheets and bed-spreads make good dust sheets, but use plastic sheeting underneath as blobs of paint can soak through fabric.

Time spent preparing the walls and surfaces is essential. Use a scraper to remove wallpaper or loose paint. Clean all surfaces with sugar soap and sand them so that they accept the paint better. Fill in any holes and cracks with filler.

When you get started on your painting be sure not to overload the brush or roller. It will start to drip and you'll be wasting paint as well as making a mess. Just dip the first third of the brush into the paint and remove the excess on the side of the tin.

Work from right to left if you are right-handed and vice versa if you are left-handed. Your arm will be away from your body.

Hammering basics

You will need a hammer whenever you want to put up a picture, pull out a loose nail or even knock down a partition wall.

→ Go for an all-purpose hammer with a metal claw head. Choose one of a medium weight. If you are hammering in a nail, angle it slightly downwards and tap in gently, holding the hammer halfway down. Then hold the hammer at its base for more power. Hit the nail around four times until it is flush with the surface.

→ Use the claw end for removing nails.

LOOK AFTER YOUR PENNIES

GET BACK ON TRACK

It's oh so easy to live beyond our means. We've been living through a long 'age of plenty' and it's had an effect on the way we think about spending. Now times are a little tougher, it's time to tighten the purse strings and think about how to save – seriously. Easier said than done! If you've been used to having whatever you want, whenever you want it – this could be a tough one. This section will help you with some easy-to-follow tips for saving your pennies and getting back on the financial track again.

USE CASH NOT CARDS

It's alarmingly easy to overspend by putting it on the plastic – until you reach your limit, or beyond. You're in the shop, you've tried it on, it looks great, you really believe you need it – you haven't got the cash, or even money in your bank account, but you know you can have it – now. By using your credit card. Why not? But come the day when your credit card bill plops onto your door mat, the amount you owe is truly scary. You didn't really need that jumper, you haven't worn it, and you're not entirely clear why you bought it – and now you've got to pay for it. If you put off paying your credit bill this month, you'll be paying high interest on top.

If you find it tough keeping your card under control, why not try to manage without it? From now on, if you want to buy something, draw the money out in cash and spend it. Simple! You'll find it actually feels a lot harder to part with cash and you'll probably find, after a very short time, that you are spending a lot less.

DON'T BE SEDUCED BY A BARGAIN

It's cheap – it's cheaper than cheap. It's madness not to buy it. Before you know it, it's in your hand, in your bag, in your car and in your home. After a few days of just sitting there, you wonder why you were crazy enough to fall for it. You've spent money you might have saved, just because… So think carefully before you buy anything, and especially if it's marked 'reduced'. It's not a bargain if you need not have bought it at all!

Green Granny's thrifty tips

✎ Write shopping lists. Then, when you are in the shop, just buy what's on that list – nothing else. You'll save your pennies, and feel virtuous into the bargain.

✎ Choose your week's menu and research the ingredients before you go shopping, so that you don't buy too much of everything. It's very wasteful to buy a packet of something you are only going to use part of, only to have to throw the remainder away a few weeks later.

✎ If you love going to the pricier supermarkets, try buying the same things in one of the cheaper ones. You'll save pounds.

✎ If you live in a city, buy your fresh food at street markets – they are so much cheaper than supermarkets. You'll also be able to pick up bargains at the end of the day, when things are being sold off cheaply.

KEEP A SPENDING DIARY

Write down everything you spend (yes, even coffees you pick up on the way to work) as well as everything you earn and keep your record as a diary (buy or make a special note-book). You'll soon see whether you are spending beyond your means. Try cutting out the little things (odd impulse buys such as makeup or skinny lattes – they all add up).

DON'T GO SHOPPING

The more you go shopping, the more you buy. Are you relying on shopping as a leisure activity? Is shopping a social activity for you? Shopping with friends is a great way to part you from your money – everyone has a view on what suits you and they may be indulging in 'vicarious shopping' (this is where your friend gets you to spend your money instead of her own!). If you don't know what you want, don't go in the first place (even 'window shopping' is dangerous – 'just looking' can so easily morph into 'just buying'). Most shops are full of stuff you didn't know you didn't want. Ignore all the baloney about 'shopping therapy'. Make something instead (even if it's only soup) – far more satisfying. Yummy!

PIGGY BANKS ARE IN

Did you keep your pocket money in a piggy bank when you were a kid? Well, now's the time to dig it out of the attic. If it's already gone to the charity shop why not keep a big jar for everyone to put their loose change into? It's amazing how quickly it mounts up. When the jar's full, give the contents to your favourite charity or use it to treat your family or yourself.

LESS IS MORE

Learn to love the simpler life. Possessions can be a responsibility and half the time things are easier if you only have a few. The fewer you have, the more you love them. See if you can last six months without buying new clothes. If you're used to having what you want, when you want it, this could be tough. But you'll soon get used to it and notice the difference when credit card bills come in.

DON'T BUY ONLINE

It's far too easy to buy things online. You're just a few clicks away from anything your heart could desire. And it could be delivered to your home within hours. How tempting is that?

Cut your heating bills

There's an old-fashioned way to economize on your heating bills – wear more clothes! Put on layers – and some cosy socks. Try adding a vest, a sweater, and maybe even a body-warmer. Even if you're sitting still, you'll soon find you don't need to have the heating on. Just save your central heating for early mornings and the evenings. Keep a cosy throw on your sofa (see page 57) so that you can snuggle up warmly. Or you can use a hot-water bottle or millet-filled cushion heated in a microwave. If you're still too chilly – get more active. If your work involves sitting, get up and walk around regularly to get your circulation going. Put sheets of foil-covered cardboard down the backs of radiators to reflect heat and avoid placing furniture in front of them or heat will be blocked from the room.

HAPPINESS IS RECYCLING

Recycling is the thing these days. It's no longer acceptable to just throw everything you've finished with into your trusty dustbin – the planet just won't stand for it! All that waste, thanks to our excessive consumption, has meant that there is no longer anywhere to dispose of it, and the energy that is spent producing the goods in the first place is just too precious to waste on things that are used for a little while, only to be thrown out. It's time to consider how waste could be cut down. Not only could we consume less, but the things we no longer need could be passed on to someone else to use. Less waste, fewer new products, less energy consumption equals a happy planet!

CAN YOU REUSE IT YOURSELF?

But before you actually get rid of your things, are there ways you could reuse them yourself?

🐝 Use the plastic bags from shops to put your rubbish in.

🐝 'Felt' old woollies in the washing machine, cut them up into squares and restitch them into a colourful throw (see page 57).

🐝 Instead of throwing away or recycling used plastic bottles, use them again and again to carry your drinking water around with you. Some are small enough to fit neatly into your handbag.

🐝 Hang on to old tins – you can save water and gas by using them as mini-saucepans for boiling eggs in.

🐝Cut up old perished hot-water bottles into squares – use them to stand mixing bowls on, to prevent them slipping.

CHOOSE TO REFUSE

Everything you buy seems to come wrapped up several times over. Why should four apples be sold in a cleverly moulded container, which is then wrapped tightly in plastic, then placed in a plastic bag? It's not only wasteful of resources, but totally unnecessary. Instead, buy your apples loose.

When you get to the supermarket checkout, does the friendly till operator automatically reach for a plastic bag to put your shopping into? Why not make your own 'bag for life' (see page 52) and take it with you when you go shopping. Within a very short time you'll be saving a whole lot of plastic bags.

GREEN GRANNY SAYS...

"If everyone reused, refused and recycled – together we could really make a difference!"

How to make your own
Bag for life

Take this special bag with you wherever you go. Choose colourful remnants and dressmaking scraps. If you like, make a patchwork version. Try making several – one to go in your handbag, one to put in the car and one hanging in the hall or kitchen – that way you'll never be without one and you won't need plastic bags ever again.

1 Cut out two pieces of fabric to 46 x 51cm (18 x 20in). Place them right sides together and tack along the two sides and the bottom, leaving enough to make a seam allowance. Machine stitch. Fold the top edge over twice and topstitch in place.

2 Use ready-made webbing for the handles. Cut two to your required length (about 38cm/15in). Tack in place on either side of the bag opening and machine stitch in place, forming a strong rectangle of stitching. Then stitch across the rectangle from corner to corner. If you want the bag to close, add a button and loop.

SOCIABLE RECYCLING

Recycling doesn't have to be a solitary pursuit. Get together with friends and pool your ideas. Recycling will be more fun that way.

🐝 Do you find your kids get bored with their toys after a while? Don't be tempted to go out and buy new ones. An easy way to ring the changes is to swap toys with friends. Some local authorities have toy libraries you can use in the same way.

🐝 Get together with friends and swap books with them. Agree a date for returning. It's much better than buying new and great to get recommendations from people you know.

🐝 Take plant cuttings and swap them with your friends. This way, you'll get a whole lot more variety in your garden or window box.

🐝 If you've ever fancied your friends' clothes, but are too skint to afford them yourself, you could try doing swaps – either for keeps, or on the understanding that you return them at a later date.

What to do with your recyclables

There are plenty of ways of passing on your recyclables – choose whatever suits you best. Use:

→ Your local charity shop, such as Oxfam.

→ Your local authority recycling centre (for larger items and things that can't be sold or given to anyone).

→ School sales, bazaars and fund-raisers.

→ Jumble sales.

→ Car boot sales and garage sales.

→ eBay selling.

→ Your local authority recycling collection (for normal household waste, organic waste, recyclable cardboard, bottles, tins, plastic bags and bottles – these vary from one district to another).

→ Some local authorities will collect old white goods from your home.

→ Local schemes for passing on goods to others or swapping.

CHARITY SHOPS ARE IT!

Charity shops, such as Oxfam, make a huge contribution towards the community recycling effort, reducing the amount of stuff that gets thrown away and put into landfill sites. They help the community in a number of ways: they raise money for a good cause, they help people get rid of unwanted possessions and they help people buy goods and clothes at very reasonable prices.

HOW TO GIVE TO A CHARITY SHOP

Usually you can just take your bag of goodies along to the shop and they'll gratefully take it from you. Call first if you think they might not accept a particular item. Things to consider:

🐝 Charity shops, such as Oxfam, sell items that have a second life. So make sure that things you give are clean and work properly. Charities spend large amounts of money that they cannot afford disposing of broken bric-a-brac, which they cannot sell. A good way of deciding whether an object is good enough to donate is to ask yourself, 'Would I buy it?'

🐝 Reusing is even better than recycling – remember that you are supporting a good cause and helping the environment.

🐝 If you can't deliver your items to the shop, fill a charity shop collection sack or take clothes to clothing banks. Some shops may be able to collect from your home.

🐝 Check the shop can accept electrical goods or furniture first.

🐝 Check before taking unusual items such as a bicycle, computer, medical equipment, sewing machines, spectacles and tools.

🐝 Don't forget. The next time you need to buy something new, why not try looking in a charity shop before going to a 'normal' shop? They need you to buy and they need you to donate too!

HOW TO BUY FROM CHARITY SHOPS

The technique for finding goodies in charity shops is to go often to check new arrivals. Of course there's no obligation to buy until you find exactly what you want. Some shops (like Oxfam) are willing to note what you want and put the item aside for you. You can also take things back if you're not satisfied (keep your receipt).

- Fabric remnants
  & scraps
- Scissors
- Sewing machine
- Sewing thread
- Needles & pins
- Backing fabric
- Cotton batting
- Seam binding

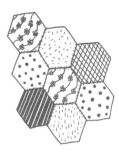

How to make a
Memory quilt

If you've got a stash of old clothes that you no longer wear – perhaps even childhood or teenage items that you haven't had the heart to get rid of – why not think of making them into a wonderful patchwork memory quilt? Every time you snuggle up under it you can remember times gone by. Use your lovely quilt on your bed for really cosy nights, give it away as a special gift, or arrange it on your sofa – great for hiding worn patches!

1 Cut the fabric into squares, hexagons, or whatever shape you are using, as big or small as you want. It's a good idea to choose similar fabrics, such as cottons, so that some squares are not heavier than others.

2 Lay all the pieces out on a flat surface. Arrange the colours in a pleasing way. Machine-stitch or hand-sew them all together to make one quilt top. Press flat.

3 Attach a backing fabric. You can make the quilt thicker by inserting a layer of batting between the quilt top and backing. Stitch through all three layers. Bind the edges with contrasting ribbon or tape.

4 Quilt the layers together by stitching through at intervals. You can embellish these corners by sewing on beads, found shells, and, for a quirky touch, even bits of driftwood.

5 Bind the edges with seam binding or ribbon of a contrasting colour, all the way round.

How to make an old
Sweater throw

If your evenings get a little chilly, try making this snug throw. Simply collect up old woollies you no longer want, felt them and make a truly original patchwork throw.

You Will Need

- Old sweaters
- Scissors
- Sewing machine
- Sewing thread
- Backing fabric
- Trimmings

1 Felt the sweaters by putting them in the washing machine on a high temperature. Experiment to see what temperature works.

2 Cut squares out of the felted wool and stitch them together, by hand or machine, to make a patchwork.

3 Back the throw with fleece fabric (purchased from fabric supply shops) or an old travel rug. Stitch the layers together at the corners of each square. You can add funky buttons or colourful tufts of embroidery thread if you like.

~ chapter 2 ~

Yummy food for less

There are loads of ways of eating
more cheaply. You could be saving your pennies
by shopping more carefully, growing your own
food and maybe even foraging for wild food. Also
you could be cooking more thriftily and making
the best use of leftovers. There's really no need
to throw any food away – and you'll
be healthier too.

BE SURE TO ALWAYS SHOP WISE

Have you ever thought about your food-shopping habits? Is it a case of rushing into the nearest supermarket on the way home to grab something tempting? Just a little thought could give you a better diet, be lighter on your purse and improve your health too.

A LITTLE FORWARD PLANNING

Some people sit down once a week and sort next week's menu. Well, they could teach the rest of us a few tricks! It makes sense to balance your nutritional intake and it's a good idea to shop for what you need, when you need it. That way, you won't buy too much, cook too much or throw precious food away. If you do have leftovers, you can eat them another day and you can even turn them into other dishes (see page 85).

Box schemes

What a great idea! A big box of locally grown, organic, in-season fruit and veggies turns up on your doorstep every week without you having to even think about it – and you get the chance to revisit your cookery books to dream up exciting, nutritious meals to use up the contents. On top of this, you may well receive things in your box that you have never tried before and have never thought of buying, so it gives you the chance to experiment, experiment, experiment.

Shop locally, in season

Shopping locally is a great way to get your food fresh and in peak condition. The same stuff might be cheaper in the supermarket, but much of it will have been flown in and be pretty tasteless to boot. If you buy food in season, it will be far cheaper and will usually have been grown locally. It'll be ripe for eating – ideal if you want to buy quantities for bottling or freezing.

Choosing the best

PRODUCE Look for plump fruit and veggies and avoid wilted green leaves and wrinkled skins. Potatoes and onions should feel hard and tomatoes should be firm. Don't buy bruised fruit, though a few blemishes are quite OK. Fruit should have some scent.

MEAT Many people are turning vegetarian, or even vegan, these days and it makes good sense for your pocket and the planet to cut down meat consumption. When you do buy meat, make sure it's the best you can afford. Beef should be plum-red and slightly moist. Lamb and pork should be pale pink, firm and smooth. Chicken should have a plump white breast and smooth legs.

FISH Make sure fish is absolutely fresh. The flesh must be firm and even-textured. Fish should have clear, shiny eyes, bright-red gills and a clean, sea smell. Avoid eating over-fished species (these vary) and eat locally caught fish, if possible.

GROW GREAT NOSH

If you've got green fingers, or even if you haven't, you might like to have a go at growing your own food. You don't have to have a vast garden – complete with vegetable patch – to achieve this, just a modest space will do and if you live in a flat, try starting up a window box. Alternatively, a small, sheltered patio may be just right for a few pots of herbs.

STARTING SMALL

If you're not an experienced gardener, but you'd like to try growing food, start with a couple of easy projects. You can quickly and easily grow your own sprouts in the kitchen and a small herb collection on your windowsill will give you much satisfaction.

HERB WINDOWSILL PROJECT

The four best herbs to grow in your kitchen are mint, chives, basil and parsley.

Mint is great to grow from cuttings, so if your friends or neighbours already have some, ask them if they can spare one. You just put a stem into water for a while and it roots by itself.

Chives will carry on for a few years, but you can put them in a potting shed over the winter.

Basil is an annual, but will keep going for a while if you take leaves from the top.

Parsley is a great herb to have as you can use it in so many recipes. Sometimes you can stall flowering by cutting it right back.

Grow your own
Sprouting seeds

Beans and sprouting seeds are highly nutritious and cheap to grow and they make delicious additions to your salads.

You Will Need

- Glass jar
- Old tights
- Seeds (such as mung beans & chickpeas)
- Elastic band

1 Fill a glass jar half full of water and put two teaspoonfuls of seeds in. Leave overnight. Stretch a piece of old tights over the top and fix with an elastic band. Rinse and drain a couple of times and leave to drain upside down.

2 Repeat this rinsing and draining, several times a day, for three days. The seeds will start sprouting in five to seven days.

GREEN GRANNY SAYS...

"Have a go at growing your own. Food tastes terrific when you have grown, nurtured, picked and cooked it yourself!"

ALLOTMENTS ARE THE THING!

Allotments are all the rage these days. Though they've existed for hundreds of years, they really took off providing food during WW2. Now they're in demand all around the country. Waiting lists may mean you can't get hold of one straight away, but there may be other initiatives, such as 'land-share' schemes, whereby you can 'borrow' land to grow your own food. Perhaps you know of someone in your neighbourhood who might let you use part of their garden.

Apart from the satisfaction of digging your own spuds and eating yummy baked-potato suppers, you'll be thinking about saving pennies. But you'll also be growing food in season and it'll be totally organic. Do your own composting, plan crop rotation and avoid gluts by staggering plantings.

Things to grow

As you gain experience you'll be wanting to try out new things to take back to the kitchen to cook and eat. This list gives a range of the easier-to-grow foods:

✔ Beetroot	✔ Leeks	✔ Radishes
✔ Broad beans	✔ Lettuce	✔ Rhubarb
✔ Brussels sprouts	✔ Onions	✔ Runner beans
✔ Cabbage	✔ Peas	✔ Spinach
✔ Celery	✔ Parsnips	✔ Swedes
	✔ Potatoes	✔ Tomatoes

GOOD THINGS TO GATHER

There is an amazing variety of foods you can gather yourself from wild places, at no cost. Mushrooms are popular with foragers, but you need a good identification guide to help you gather the ones that aren't poisonous, so they aren't included here. This list is a short sample of the sorts of foods you can pick to eat or drink – of course there are many more on offer. When you choose to eat wild food, always make sure that you are confident about what you are eating; never take a chance on it. If in doubt, consult an expert first.

Dandelions Gather the roots to make coffee. Twenty-five small roots are enough for one cup.

Nettles Use all parts of the plant to make the tea. Or you can use the leaves in soups, risottos and beers.

Wild garlic The bulbs are edible and the leaves are delicious both raw and cooked.

Blackberries These are great raw or made into scrumptious crumbles. They make a good partner with apples.

Marsh samphire This is known as 'poor man's asparagus' and is found on salt marshes.

Elder This fast-growing shrub provides two edible possibilities. The flowers can be made into cordials and the berries can be made into pies, jellies and wines.

Sea beet is found on banks and sea shingle and you can use it just like ordinary spinach.

Sweet violets are reasonably common in hedgerows and their delicate, blue flowers can be used in salads and to flavour rice puddings.

GREEN GRANNY'S FOOD TIPS

There are lots of simple hints and tips about food that you really need to know if you're going to be green and thrifty in the kitchen. And they're all very simple too. When you are preparing, storing or freezing food or if you need some basic advice on making jams and preserves, these pages are sure to help you.

PROPER PREPARATION & COOKING

There are a few useful things to be aware of when you are preparing your food:

🍴 When you are boiling water, use the pan lid. Heat won't escape and your water will boil more quickly – you'll save energy.

🍴 Why not steam your food? By using a steamer that stacks over saucepans, you can use the same energy for cooking two items, and the steamed veggies will hold their nutritional value better. You can buy electric steamers with up to four stacked containers, so that you can steam a range of foods all at once.

🍴 When you are preparing fruit and veggies beware of throwing good bits away. For example, scrub potatoes and carrots rather than peeling them.

🍴 Eat all of your lettuce. Just wash it and then pat dry. If you do need to discard bits and pieces, put them in your compost bin.

🍴 Slow cookers are a great way to save energy. They apply a small amount of heat over a long period. You just put everything in in the morning and when you get back, hungry and tired, there's a delicious hot meal waiting for you. You can use cheaper cuts of meat because the slow cooking softens the fibres.

🐝 Microwaves save time and energy. If you want to eat a dish from frozen, you can defrost it quickly and heat it as usual. Just make sure that all your food is piping hot before you serve it.

🐝 Eggs are quick and nutritious when you don't have time to make something more elaborate.

Eggy solutions

- ✔ Poached
- ✔ Boiled
- ✔ French toast
- ✔ Fried

- ✔ Baked
- ✔ Hard-boiled
- ✔ Scrambled
- ✔ Scotch

- ✔ Stuffed
- ✔ Curried
- ✔ Omelette

SENSIBLE STORAGE

Storage needs to be simple and safe. A few easy guidelines will keep your food fresh and you'll feel confident about eating it.

🐝 There's no need to use expensive clingfilm and foil to protect leftovers in the fridge. Just cover the bowl with a plate or tea towel.

🐝 'Sell by' and 'use by' dates are sensible, but sometimes over-zealous. Use smell, touch and taste to see if food can be eaten, but if in doubt, don't take a chance on food past its use-by date.

🐝 When you are storing fruit and veggies, keep them in a cool, airy place, such as a larder or the veggie compartment of your fridge. Don't store carrots and apples next to each other as the carrots will acquire a bitterness. Potatoes will spoil if they are stored next to onions. Cut leaves from root veggies before you store them, to prevent sap rising. It's nice to arrange fruit in a bowl, but keep bananas separately as they cause other fruit to ripen too rapidly.

🦞 If you don't eat everything you've ordered in a restaurant, no need to waste the food, ask for a doggy bag and have it the next day.

FREEZING FRENZY

Here are a few freezing ideas to save time, money and energy:

🦞 If you make purée for your baby, make enough for several 'meals' and freeze the spare quantity in an ice-cube tray.

🦞 If you grow your own herbs, freeze small amounts in water in an ice-cube tray and then just use them as you need them.

🦞 Slice and freeze fresh lemon for gin and tonics and pancakes as they go mouldy quickly in the fridge drawer.

COOK TO FREEZE

Your freezer is a boon. When you cook a favourite recipe, make up double quantities and then freeze half to have at a later date. Make sure you label everything (what it is and the date you put it in).

Life in the freezer

✔ Biscuits – 6 months

✔ Bread – 4 weeks

✔ Cakes – 6 months

✔ Meat dishes – 2 months

✔ Pancakes – 2 months

✔ Pizzas (baked) – 2 months

✔ Sauces, soups, stocks –
   2–3 months

✔ Scones – 6 months

✔ Meat loaves, patés,
   terrines – 1 month

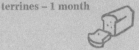

How to defrost the freezer

You should try to do this every six months. Up-to-date freezers are self-defrosting – lucky you!

➜ Remove all packages and wrap well in newspaper.

➜ Turn off electricity and place bowls of boiling water in the cabinet to speed up thawing.

➜ Scrape ice off when it becomes loose.

➜ Wipe clean with a cloth dipped in a solution of bicarbonate of soda or vinegar and water to remove stale smells.

➜ Turn electricity back on to maximum and replace packages.

How to make perfect
Roast potatoes

No roast dinner is complete without potatoes, so if you've ever wondered how to make scrumptious roasties – look no further!

1 Peel and cut potatoes into evenly sized pieces. Parboil for ten minutes and drain well. Shake them after draining to rough up the edges slightly.

2 Heat a roasting tin containing lard or sunflower oil for about five minutes or until the lard or oil is very hot. Place potatoes in it, turning them over in the oil and then sprinkle with sea salt.

3 Roast near the top of a preheated oven, 210°C (425°F) for 40 minutes, turning every now and then.

How to cook perfect
Boiled white rice

If you don't possess a rice cooker, here's what you do.

1 Use 600ml (1pt) of water and 1 tsp salt to each 50g (2oz) rice. Measure the water into a large pan and bring to the boil. Boil the rice rapidly for 12–15 minutes, or until soft.

2 Drain the rice into a sieve and rinse under warm water. Return it to the pan with a knob of butter and toss. Cover the pan for ten minutes to dry, shaking occasionally.

GREEN GRANNY'S PRESERVES

Go to a pick-your-own farm to gather soft fruit in the summer or buy it cheaply and in season from your greengrocer. You'll be able to get plenty of fruit for a very reasonable price, or if the greengrocer has a glut of fruit to sell off cheaply – go for it!

How to make
Strawberry jam

A truly delicious accompaniment for your lovely home-made scones (and cream!).

1 Hull, wash and drain the strawberries. Layer with the sugar in a large bowl. Cover with a cloth and leave in a cool place for 24 hours.

2 Put the strawberries in a pan and boil for five minutes. Leave them in the pan for 48 hours, then boil for 20 minutes or until the setting point is reached. To test, put a teaspoonful on a cold saucer. As the jam cools a skin forms. If the skin crinkles when pushed with a finger, setting point has been reached.

3 Remove scum from the finished jam. Pour into dry, heated jars and cover with a disk of waxed paper dipped in brandy or sherry to seal. Put cellophane covers on top.

You Will Need

- 1.8kg (4lb) strawberries
- 1.8kg (4lb) granulated sugar
- Sterilized jars
- Waxed paper disks
- Cellophane covers
- Elastic bands
- Labels

- 1.3kg (3lb)
  Seville oranges
- Juice of 2 lemons
- 2.7kg (6lb)
  preserving sugar
- 3.4 litres (6pt)
  water
- Sterilized jars
- Waxed paper disks
- Cellophane covers
- Elastic bands
- Labels

How to make
Seville marmalade

Buy Sevilles in bulk from your local street market or greengrocers. They'll be a real bargain. If you don't eat all the marmalade yourself, wrap the pots up prettily – they make terrific Christmas presents.

1 Peel off the orange rind in thin strips. Put it in a pan with half the water and the strained lemon juice. Bring to the boil and simmer, covered, over low heat for two hours, until the peel is tender.

2 Meanwhile, chop the peeled oranges and put them in another pan with the rest of the water. Bring to the boil, cover with a lid, and simmer the fruit for 1½ hours.

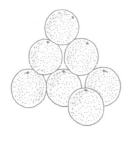

3 Strain the liquid from the orange pulp through a fine sieve into the pan with the soft peel. Bring the mixture to the boil and reduce a little before stirring in the sugar. Boil rapidly until set. Skim and leave to stand for 30 minutes, stirring occasionally. Pour into warmed, dry jars and cover with waxed paper disks. Seal the jars when cool with metal tops or clear cellophane before securing with rubber bands. Add a label.

How to make
Apple chutney

Chutney makes a wonderful feast when you serve it with home-made bread and local cheeses. Add salad for a traditional ploughman's lunch. You can buy apples cheaply in bulk when they are in season, from the greengrocer, farmer's market or your local street market.

1 Peel, core and chop the apples and put them in a large pan.

2 Cook with 236ml (½pt) of vinegar and the crushed garlic until thick and pulpy.

3 Add the remaining vinegar, the sugar, ginger, mixed spice, a good pinch of cayenne and salt. Continue cooking for a further 20 minutes or until thick. Pot and cover with waxed disk and cellophane. Secure with elastic bands.

You Will Need

- 1.8kg (4lb) cooking apples
- 600ml (1pt) vinegar
- 2-3 cloves garlic
- 680g (1½lb) soft brown sugar
- 113g (4oz) crystallized ginger
- ½ level tsp mixed spice
- cayenne pepper
- ½ level tsp salt
- Sterilized jars
- Waxed paper disks
- Cellophane covers
- Elastic bands
- Labels

GREEN GRANNY'S RECIPES

You may well have got stuck in a bit of a 'recipe-rut'. It happens! You've got a nice collection of recipe books, but have you noticed how you always turn to the same old recipes? This selection helps you plan carefully and get the most from the food you grow and buy. It gives you new ideas for using up store cupboard favourites, meals you can prepare in minutes when you haven't got much time, delicious ways of using up leftovers and surpluses and how to cook one-pot recipes.

Now that you are thinking of broadening your cooking skills, this chapter offers you a refresher course in simple, affordable, and most importantly, delicious, recipes to try out. They're all quick and easy, so no more excuses and wails of 'I'm a hopeless cook!' Your friends and relatives will soon be flocking to eat at your table.

GET YOUR FIVE A DAY

Five portions of fruit and veggies a day is a good number to aim for, but more is even better to get all the nutrients your body needs. Think of eating a 'rainbow' range of vegetable and fruit colours: red, orange, purple, yellow and green – you'll get maximum nutritional benefits that way.

STORE CUPBOARD GOODIES

There's no need to make a dash for the shops when you think there's no food in the house. Just take a look in your store cupboard and see if you can rustle up a simple meal with what you already have.

Special homemade
Beans on toast

Try this new take on an old standby. It's so delicious that it'll become one of your regular quick meals.

Preparation time: 5 minutes
Cooking time: 25 minutes
Serves: 2–3

1 Heat the oil in a saucepan and fry the onion and celery for 5 minutes until golden. Blend the cornflour with 2 tablespoons water and add to the pan along with the remaining ingredients.

2 Bring the mixture to the boil, reduce the heat slightly and cook, with the lid off, for about 20 minutes, stirring frequently, until the mixture is thickened and pulpy. Pile on toast to serve.

You Will Need

- 2 tbsp veg oil
- 1 onion, chopped
- 1 celery stick, thinly sliced
- 1 tsp cornflour
- 425g (14oz) can cannellini beans
- 250g (8oz) tin chopped tomatoes
- 300ml (½pt) veg stock
- 1 tbsp coarse-grain mustard
- 1 tbsp black treacle
- 1 tbsp ketchup
- 1 tbsp Worcestershire sauce
- Salt & pepper

- 250g (8oz) macaroni
- 4 slices bacon, fried
- 1 garlic clove, crushed
- 120ml (4fl oz) single cream
- 120ml (4fl oz) milk
- Pinch of freshly grated nutmeg
- 150g (5oz) hard cheese, such as cheddar or Gruyère, grated
- 4 tbsp chopped basil
- Salt & pepper

Marvellous
Macaroni cheese

This old favourite is a great quick supper when you fancy some cheery comfort food.

Preparation time: 5 minutes
Cooking time: 20 minutes
Serves: 4

1 Cook the macaroni in a pan of lightly salted boiling water for 10–12 minutes, until tender but still firm to the bite. Drain and place in a large bowl.

2 Meanwhile, fry the bacon in a small frying pan until browned but not crisp. Add the garlic, sauté for a minute and then add the cream and milk and season with a little nutmeg. Bring just to the boil.

3 Stir in 100g (3½oz) of the cheese and all the basil, remove from the heat and stir until the cheese melts. Season to taste with salt and pepper and stir into the macaroni.

4 Arrange in an ovenproof dish, top with the remaining cheese and bake in a preheated oven, 230°C (450°F), Gas Mark 8, for 10 minutes or until golden.

Tasty
Falafel cakes

These tasty chickpea cakes, traditionally rolled into little balls and deep-fried, make a great veggie supper served simply with a fresh, Greek-style salad.

Preparation time: 10 minutes
Cooking time: 10 minutes
Serves: 4

1 Place the chickpeas in a food processor or blender with the onion, garlic, spices, herbs, breadcrumbs and a little salt and pepper. Blend briefly to make a chunky paste.

2 Take dessertspoonfuls of the mixture and flatten into cakes. Heat a 1cm (½in) depth of oil in a frying pan and fry half the falafel for about 3 minutes, turning once until crisp and golden. Drain on kitchen paper and keep warm while cooking the remainder.

- 2 garlic cloves, crushed
- 2 x 400g (14oz) tins chopped tomatoes
- 4 tbsp extra virgin olive oil
- 1 tsp dried oregano
- 1 tsp sugar
- 8 slices of bacon, finely chopped
- 75g (3oz) mascarpone cheese or 6 tbsp crème fraîche
- Salt & pepper
- Pasta, to serve

Tomato & bacon
Pasta sauce

This is a good basic sauce for pasta and it can be made without the bacon for vegetarians. It's a good idea to make up several batches, minus the mascarpone or crème fraîche, and freeze it for future use.

Preparation time: 3 minutes
Cooking time: 15 minutes
Serves: 4

1 Put the garlic, tomatoes, oil, oregano and sugar in a saucepan. Season to taste with salt and pepper and bring to a boil, cover and simmer for 10 minutes.

2 Add the bacon and simmer, uncovered, for another 5 minutes.

3 Stir in the mascarpone or crème fraîche, heat through, then taste and adjust the seasoning if necessary. Serve with freshly cooked pasta.

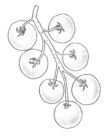

Spicy
Chilli bean soup

This hits the spot when the weather is miserable and you feel like warming your soul as well as your body. You're almost guaranteed to have the ingredients in your store cupboard.

Preparation time: 8 minutes
Cooking time: 22 minutes
Serves: 3–4

1 Heat the oil in a saucepan and sauté the onion, garlic, chilli powder, coriander and cumin, stirring frequently, for 5 minutes, or until the onion has softened. Add the beans, tomatoes and stock and season to taste with salt and pepper.

2 Bring to a boil, cover and then simmer for 15 minutes. Transfer to a food processor or blender and process until fairly smooth. Pour into heatproof bowls.

3 Place tortilla chips on top of the soup, scatter over the grated cheese and grill for 1–2 minutes or until the cheese has melted. Serve immediately with sour cream.

- 2 tbsp olive oil
- 1 onion, chopped
- 1 garlic clove, crushed
- 1 tsp chilli powder
- 1 tsp ground coriander
- 1 tsp ground cumin
- 400g (14oz) tin red kidney beans, drained
- 400g (14oz) tin chopped tomatoes
- 475ml (16fl oz) vegetable stock
- 12 tortilla chips
- 50g (2oz) grated cheddar cheese
- Salt & pepper
- Sour cream, to serve

MEALS IN MINUTES

We're all pushed for time these days, but it's important to eat well to keep healthy and happy. When you need a quick, basic meal after a hard day's work, try something from this selection of easy recipes.

You Will Need

- 12 fresh lasagne sheets
- 3 tbsp extra virgin olive oil
- 500g (1lb) mixed mushrooms (shiitake, oyster & chestnut), sliced
- 200g (7oz) mascarpone cheese
- 125g (4oz) baby spinach
- 150g (5oz) taleggio cheese, without rind and cut into cubes
- Salt & pepper

Mushroom & spinach
Lasagne

Who said lasagne was complicated? Throw this dish together for a simple supper.

Preparation time: 10 minutes
Cooking time: 15 minutes
Serves: 4

1 Place the lasagne sheets in a large roasting tray and pour over boiling water. Leave to stand for 5 minutes, then drain. Heat the oil in a frying pan and fry the mushrooms for five minutes. Add the mascarpone and turn up the heat. Cook for 1 minute, until the sauce is thick. Season.

2 Lightly oil an ovenproof dish and place three sheets of lasagne on it. Top with a little of the taleggio, one-third of the mushroom sauce and one-third of the spinach. Repeat with two more layers and top with the remaining taleggio. Grill until golden.

Buttered
Cauliflower crumble

This old favourite takes only minutes to prepare. A large baked potato makes a perfect, filling accompaniment.

Preparation time: 8 minutes
Cooking time: 12 minutes
Serves: 4

You Will Need

- 1 large cauliflower
- 25g (1oz) butter
- 50g (2oz) breadcrumbs
- 2 tbsp olive oil
- 3 tbsp capers
- 3 cocktail gherkins, finely chopped
- 3 tbsp chopped dill or tarragon
- 100g (3½oz) crème fraîche
- 4 tbsp grated Parmesan cheese
- Salt & pepper

1 Cut the cauliflower into large florets and blanch in boiling water for 2 minutes. Drain the florets thoroughly. Melt half of the butter in a large frying pan. Add the breadcrumbs and fry for 2 minutes, until golden. Drain and set aside.

2 Melt the remaining butter in the pan with the oil. Add the cauliflower florets and fry gently for about 5 minutes, until golden. Add the capers, gherkins, dill or tarragon and crème fraîche, season to taste with salt and pepper and stir the mixture over a moderate heat for 1 minute.

3 Turn into a shallow flameproof dish and sprinkle with the fried breadcrumbs and Parmesan. Cook under a preheated moderate grill for about 2 minutes.

- 3 red peppers,
  cored, deseeded
  and quartered
- 375g (13oz) ripe
  plum tomatoes,
  skinned
- 6 tbsp extra
  virgin olive oil
- 3 tbsp wine
  vinegar
- 2 garlic cloves,
  crushed
- 125g (4oz) stale
  ciabatta bread
- 50g (2oz) pitted
  black olives
- Small handful of
  basil leaves,
  shredded
- Salt & pepper

Punchy
Panzanella

In this Italian salad, pieces of ciabatta are tossed with the other ingredients; a great way to use up slightly stale ciabatta.

Preparation time: 15 minutes
Cooking time: 10 minutes
Serves: 4 or 2 as a main course

1 Place the peppers, skin side up, on a foil-lined grill rack and grill under a preheated moderate grill for 10 minutes or until the skins are blackened.

2 Meanwhile, quarter the tomatoes and scoop out the pulp, placing it in a sieve over a bowl to catch the juices. Set the tomato quarters aside. Press the pulp with the back of a spoon to extract as much juice as possible.

3 Beat the oil, vinegar, garlic and salt and pepper into the tomato juice. When cool enough to handle, peel the peppers and roughly slice them into a bowl with the tomato quarters. Break the bread into small chunks and add to the bowl with the olives and basil. Add the dressing and toss the ingredients together before serving.

Quick
Tuna fishcakes

Most of us have a couple of tins of tuna in the store cupboard, but sometimes the ideas about what to do with them get a bit tired. Here's a delicious recipe to try out – see if you like it.

Preparation time: 10 minutes
Cooking time: 18 minutes
Serves: 4

1 Cook the potatoes in a pan of lightly salted boiling water for 10 minutes, or until tender. Drain well, mash and cool slightly.

2 Meanwhile, flake the tuna. Beat the tuna, cheese, spring onions, garlic, thyme and egg into the mashed potatoes. Season to taste with cayenne, salt and pepper.

3 Divide the mixture into four and shape into thick patties. Dust with seasoned flour and fry in a shallow layer of vegetable oil for 5 minutes on each side, or until crisp and golden. Serve hot with a mixed green salad and mayonnaise.

You Will Need

- 250g (8oz) baking potatoes, peeled and diced
- 2 x 200g (7oz) cans tuna in olive oil, drained
- 50g (2oz) cheddar cheese, grated
- 4 spring onions, finely chopped
- 1 small garlic clove, crushed
- 2 tsp dried thyme
- 1 small egg, beaten
- ½ tsp cayenne pepper
- 4 tbsp seasoned flour
- Salt & pepper
- Vegetable oil for frying

- 4 loin pork chops, about 175g (6oz) each
- 3 parsnips, cut into chunks
- 1 butternut squash, peeled, deseeded and thickly sliced
- 2 red-skinned dessert apples, cored and quartered
- 1 tsp fennel seeds
- 2 tsp coriander seeds
- 2 garlic cloves, chopped
- 1 tsp turmeric
- 3 tbsp olive oil
- 1 tbsp clear honey
- Salt & pepper

One-pan
Spiced pork

Great for no-fuss entertaining: simply place the pork chops in a roasting tin with the other ingredients and leave them to bake, safe in the knowledge that the dinner will look after itself.

Preparation time: 15 minutes
Cooking time: 40 minutes
Serves: 4

1 Snip through the fat on the rind of the pork chops so that they do not curl up during cooking. Place them in a large roasting tin with the parsnips, squash and apples.

2 Crush the fennel and coriander seeds with a pestle and mortar, then mix with the garlic, turmeric, oil and honey. Season with salt and pepper and brush the mixture over the pork and vegetables.

3 Cook in a preheated oven, 190°C (375°F), Gas Mark 5, for 35–40 minutes, turning the vegetables once, until golden brown and tender. Spoon on to warmed plates and serve.

TWO MEALS FROM ONE

If you are already eating up your leftovers – that's really great! So many people seem to throw them away after the first meal, when they could be stored in the fridge and used again the next day. Things often taste better the second time around anyway. If you really want to be creative, why not consider making something new with your leftover dish? Here are some terrific suggestions for yummy things to do with your leftovers – for very little extra time, effort and cost.

How to make a basic
Mince-meat sauce

Use this basic recipe for a range of different dishes. Make double quantities and freeze half to use another time in a different way.

1 Heat the oil in a saucepan and add the onion and garlic. Fry until soft. Add mince and fry until brown.

2 Add tinned tomatoes, purée, basil and seasoning. Mix well and simmer for 20 minutes.

3 Serve with pasta, make into a lasagne bake or add chilli and red kidney beans for a chilli con carne.

You Will Need

- 1 tbsp olive oil
- 1 large onion, chopped
- 2 cloves of garlic, crushed
- 500g (1lb) steak mince meat
- 2 tins chopped tomatoes
- 2 tbsp tomato purée
- 1 tbsp dried basil
- Salt & pepper

- 2.5kg (5lb) piece of gammon
- 2 onions, sliced
- 2 carrots, roughly chopped
- 2 celery sticks, roughly chopped
- Sprigs of thyme
- 4 bay leaves
- 1 tbsp peppercorns
- 8 whole star anise
- 2 tbsp orange marmalade
- 75g (3oz) light muscovado sugar
- 6 kumquats, thinly sliced

Festive
Glazed ham

A large joint of gammon does well hot one day, cold the next. If you have any left over, try the variation on the right.

Preparation time: 15 minutes, plus soaking
Cooking time: 2 hours 20 mins – 3 hours
Serves: 8–12

1 Soak the joint overnight in cold water. Drain and weigh to calculate cooking time, allowing 20 minutes per 500g (1lb). Put it in a saucepan and add the onions, carrots, celery, thyme, bay leaves, peppercorns and three of the star anise. Cover with water, bring to a simmer, then cover and cook gently for the calculated time. Leave to cool for 30 minutes.

2 Drain the meat. Cut away the rind and cut diagonal lines across the fat, then score in the opposite direction. Melt the marmalade and stir in the sugar. Spread the mixture over the meat and arrange the kumquats and remaining star anise. Put it in a foil-lined tin. Cook in a preheated oven, 200°C (400°F), Gas Mark 6, for 20 minutes or until the sugar starts to caramelize. Leave to stand for 20 minutes.

Variation: Ham & Brie
Frittata

If you have any ham or gammon left over from the recipe on the left, try this delicious variation.

Preparation time: 4 minutes
Cooking time: 6 minutes
Serves: 4

You Will Need

- 6 large free-range eggs
- 2 tbsp chopped parsley
- 2 tbsp extra virgin olive oil
- 100g (4oz) piece leftover smoked ham or gammon
- 75g (3oz) Brie cheese
- Salt & pepper

1 Beat the eggs and season with parsley, salt and pepper. Heat the oil in a large, non-stick frying pan and swirl in the egg mixture.

2 Cook over medium heat for three minutes, until almost set. Meanwhile, shred the ham and thinly slice the Brie. Scatter the ham and cheese over the frittata and cook under a preheated grill for 2–3 minutes, until golden.

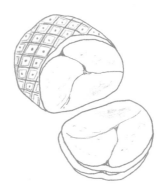

- 340g (12oz) sweet potatoes
- 1 red onion, thinly sliced
- 4 tbsp chilli-infused olive oil
- Sprigs of thyme
- 40g (1½oz) sun-dried tomatoes, thinly sliced
- 4 mackerel fillets
- Salt & pepper
- Lemon wedges to garnish

For the raita

- 100ml (3½fl oz) natural yogurt
- 1 tbsp chopped coriander
- 1 tbsp chopped mint

Sweet potatoes &
Roast mackerel

Chilli-infused olive oil adds a hot spiciness that's lovely with cooling mint raita. If you have any leftover mackerel, try the variation opposite the next day.

Preparation time: 15 minutes
Cooking time: 1 hour
Serves: 4

1 Scrub the sweet potatoes and cut into 1.5cm (¾in) chunks. Scatter the pieces in a shallow dish with the onion. Add the oil, thyme and a little salt and mix together.

2 Bake in a preheated oven, 200°C (400°F), Gas Mark 6, for 40–45 minutes, turning once or twice, until the potatoes are tender and beginning to brown. Stir in the tomatoes.

3 Fold each mackerel fillet in half, skin side out, and place on the potatoes. Return to the oven for a further 12–15 minutes or until the fish is tender. Meanwhile, mix the yogurt, herbs and a little seasoning in a serving bowl. Transfer the fish and potatoes to warm serving plates, spoon over the raita. Serve with lemon wedges.

Variation: Smoked
Mackerel kedgeree

You
Will
Need

Yesterday's mackerel (see opposite) is perfect for this classic breakfast dish.

Preparation time: 15 minutes
Cooking time: about 10 minutes
Serves: 4

1 Place the eggs in a small pan of boiling water and cook them for 7 minutes. Drain, run them under cold water, peel and cut into quarters.

2 Meanwhile, heat the butter in a frying pan, add the smoked mackerel, rice and curry powder and toss until everything is warmed through and the rice is evenly coated. Stir in the lemon juice, parsley and boiled eggs and serve immediately.

- 3 large eggs
- 25g (1oz) butter
- 375g (13oz) smoked mackerel, flaked
- 375g (13oz) cooked basmati rice
- 1 tsp mild curry powder
- 4 tbsp lemon juice
- 4 tbsp chopped parsley

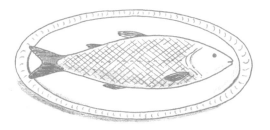

Pot roast
Chicken

This dish makes a delightful change from a traditional roast chicken. If you have any leftover chicken, try the variation opposite.

Preparation time: 15 minutes
Cooking time: 2 hours
Serves: 4

- 1.5kg (3lb) chicken
- 25g (1oz) butter
- 2 tbsp olive oil
- 1 onion, sliced
- 3 celery sticks, sliced
- 4-6 garlic cloves, crushed
- 250ml (8fl oz) dry white wine
- 3 bay leaves
- Sprigs of thyme
- 150g (5oz) puy lentils
- 2 tbsp capers
- 4 tbsp chopped parsley
- 100g (4oz) crème fraîche
- Salt & pepper

1 Season the chicken. Melt the butter with the oil in a frying pan and fry the chicken on all sides. Transfer to a large casserole.

2 Fry the onion and celery in the pan juices for 6–8 minutes, or until browned. Stir in the garlic, wine and herbs and pour over the chicken. Cover and bake in a preheated oven, 160°C (320°F), Gas Mark 3, for 1 hour.

3 Meanwhile, rinse the lentils and put them in a saucepan with plenty of water. Bring to the boil and boil for 10 minutes. Drain well. Tip the lentils around the chicken and return to the oven for a further 45 minutes. Transfer the cooked chicken to a warm dish and cover. Mix the capers, parsley and crème fraîche and heat through, stirring. Serve with the chicken.

Variation:
Jambalaya

This Creole dish is a great way of using up leftover roast chicken (see opposite).

Preparation time: 4–10 minutes
Cooking time: 22–25 minutes
Serves: 4

1 Heat the olive oil in a large frying pan and fry the onion for 3 minutes. Add the sausages and chicken and fry for a further 2 minutes.

2 Add the rice, tomatoes, peppers, chicken stock, bay leaves and allspice. Cover and simmer very gently for 10 minutes or until the rice is tender and the liquid has been absorbed. Season with salt and pepper and scatter with oregano. Serve with soured cream.

- 2 tbsp olive oil
- 1 onion
- 100g (4oz) sliced smoked sausages
- 125g (4oz) cubed leftover chicken
- 125g (4oz) quick-cook rice
- 400g (14oz) can chopped tomatoes
- 200g (7oz) chopped chargrilled peppers in oil
- 600ml (1pt) chicken stock
- 2 bay leaves
- Pinch allspice
- Salt & pepper
- Chopped oregano, to garnish
- Soured cream, to serve

You Will Need

- 4 salmon fillets, 175–250g/6–8oz each
- 4 tbsp lemon juice
- 4 tbsp olive oil
- 1 tbsp balsamic vinegar
- 1 tbsp honey
- 4 garlic cloves, finely chopped
- 2 red onions, quartered
- 2 fennel bulbs, quartered
- 16–20 cherry vine tomatoes
- Salt & pepper

Fennel, tomato &
Roast salmon

Salmon is easy to get hold of in the shops, so try this delicious basic recipe. Use any leftover salmon to make the pasta variation on the facing page.

Preparation time: 10 minutes
Cooking time: 25 minutes
Serves: 4

1 Season the salmon fillets generously with salt and pepper and pour the lemon juice over them. Set aside.

2 In a small bowl, combine the olive oil, balsamic vinegar, honey and garlic, and season with salt and pepper. Put the onion, fennel and tomatoes in a bowl and pour over the oil mixture. Toss to coat thoroughly, then spread on a baking sheet. Place in a preheated oven, 220°C (425°F), Gas Mark 7, and roast for 10 minutes. Add the salmon fillets to the baking sheet and roast for a further 12–15 minutes. Serve with the roasted vegetables and rice or couscous.

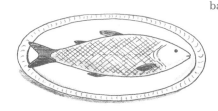

Variation: Pesto &
Salmon pasta

If you have any salmon left over from your roast (see opposite), make this easy pasta dish the next day.

Preparation time: 10 minutes
Cooking time: 20 minutes
Serves: 4

1 Cook the pasta in plenty of lightly salted boiling water for about 8–10 minutes until almost tender.

2 Meanwhile, heat the oil in a frying pan, add the onion and fry for about 5 minutes until softened. Drain the salmon and discard skin and bones. Flake the flesh.

3 Add the peas to the pasta and cook for a further 3 minutes. Drain the pasta and peas, retaining a few tablespoons of the cooking water, and return to the pan.

4 Stir in the pesto, lemon juice, Parmesan, onion, water and flaked salmon. Season lightly with salt and pepper and toss gently. Serve immediately, topped with more Parmesan and accompanied by a leafy salad.

You Will Need

- 325g (11oz) dried penne
- 2 tbsp olive oil
- 1 onion, thinly sliced
- 400g (14oz) salmon
- 150g (5oz) frozen peas
- 2 tbsp pesto
- 1 tbsp lemon juice
- 25g (1oz) Parmesan
- Salt & pepper

- 400g (14oz) each carrots & parsnips
- 300g (10oz) sweet potatoes
- 250g (8oz) small turnips
- 250g (8oz) whole shallots or baby onions, peeled
- 2 tsp finely chopped rosemary
- 6 tbsp veg oil
- 4 tsp grainy mustard
- Finely grated rind of 1 orange, plus 3 tbsp juice
- 1 tbsp clear honey
- 1 tbsp lemon juice
- Salt & pepper

Orange & mustard glaze with
Roast veggies

Roasted root vegetables make a delicious alternative to roast potatoes. If you have any left over, try the soup recipe opposite.

Preparation time: 20 minutes
Cooking time: 1 hour 20 minutes
Serves: 4

1 Halve the carrots and parsnips lengthways and cut them into wedges. Cut the sweet potatoes into chunks. Peel and cut the turnips into wedges.

2 Bring a large saucepan of water to the boil, tip in the vegetables and cook for five minutes. Drain and transfer them to a roasting tin. Scatter with the shallots or baby onions and the rosemary. Drizzle with the oil and toss gently. Roast in a preheated oven, 200°C (400°F), Gas Mark 6, for 45 minutes.

3 Meanwhile, mix the mustard, orange rind and juice, honey, lemon juice and a little seasoning. Drizzle over the vegetables and turn until coated in the glaze. Return to the oven and roast for a further 20–30 minutes, turning occasionally, until deep golden.

Variation:
Roast veggie soup

Use up any leftover veggies from yesterday (see opposite) to make this delicious soup.

Preparation time: 5 minutes
Cooking time: 10 minutes
Serves: 4

1 Put the vegetables into a food processor. Add half the stock and process until smooth. Blend in the remaining stock.

2 Transfer to a saucepan and heat gently for 10 minutes. Season to taste,

GREEN GRANNY SAYS...

"There are loads of ways of using up leftover veggies, but this soup is truly delicious."

GLUTS & SURPLUSES

Whether you want to create something new with Sunday's leftover chicken or you've bought a job lot of tomatoes at the end of the day at the market, here are some recipes to give you inspiration.

You Will Need

- 4 ripe bananas, mashed
- 300g (10oz) self-raising flour
- 2 tbsp caster sugar
- 2 tbsp melted butter
- 100ml (3½fl oz) milk
- 1 egg, lightly beaten
- 2 tsp crushed cardamom seeds
- Sunflower oil, for brushing

Banana & cardamom
Pancakes

Banana and cardamom are an unbeatable combination, so if you've bought a lot of cheap, ripe bananas, this is for you!

Preparation time: 10 minutes
Cooking time: 10–15 minutes
Serves: 4

1 Put the bananas, flour, sugar, butter, milk and egg into a large mixing bowl and beat until smooth. Stir in the cardamom.

2 Heat a large, non-stick frying pan and brush with oil. Pour in three to four tablespoonfuls of the batter and cook for 2–3 to three minutes. Flip the pancakes and cook for another 2 minutes, or until lightly browned. Remove the pancakes and keep warm. Repeat with the remaining batter until all the pancakes are cooked. Serve with vanilla ice cream and honey.

Toffee
Apple bake

A great standby that few can resist in the autumn, when apples are freely available and you may have lots to use up. This bake is perfect served with vanilla ice cream.

Preparation Time: 10 minutes
Cooking time: 20 minutes
Serves: 4

1 Toss the apples in a shallow ovenproof dish with one tablespoonful of the flour and the muscovado sugar.

2 Mix the remaining flour with the caster sugar and mixed spice in a bowl. Add the egg, yogurt and butter and stir lightly until only just combined.

3 Spoon the mixture over the prepared apples and bake in a preheated oven, 220°C (425°F), Gas Mark 7, for about 15–20 minutes, until just firm and golden. Serve warm.

You Will Need

- 3 dessert apples, cored and thickly sliced
- 100g (4oz) self-raising flour, plus 1 tbsp extra
- 100g (4oz) light muscovado sugar
- 50g (2oz) caster sugar
- ½ tsp ground mixed spice
- 1 egg
- 100ml (4fl oz) natural yogurt
- 50g (2oz) unsalted butter, melted

You Will Need

- 150g (5oz) plain dark chocolate, broken into pieces
- 250g (8oz) leftover bread, thinly sliced
- 50g (2oz) butter, at room temperature
- 3 eggs
- 50g (2oz) caster sugar
- 1 tsp vanilla essence
- Large pinch of ground cinnamon
- 450ml (1pt) full-fat milk
- Single cream, to serve

Chocolate bread & butter
Pudding

A scrumptious way of using up any stale bread you may have (if you haven't already fed it to the ducks).

Preparation time: 15 minutes
Cooking time: 40 minutes
Serves: 4

1 Melt the chocolate in a heatproof bowl over a saucepan of gently simmering water. Spread the bread with some of the butter, adding the remainder to the chocolate.

2 Cover the bottom of a greased 1.5-litre (3-pint) ovenproof dish with a layer of bread and butter. Stir the chocolate, then spoon a little over the bread. Continue layering until you reach the top of the dish.

3 Whisk the eggs, sugar, vanilla, cinnamon and milk together, then pour over the bread and butter. Cover loosely with buttered foil and leave to stand for 15 minutes. Cook in a preheated oven, 180°C (350°F), Gas Mark 4, for 35 minutes or until the custard has set, removing the foil for the last 5 minutes to brown the top. Serve with cream.

Green Granny's
Bread pudding

If you've still got some leftover bread try this delicious traditional pud recipe. It's sure to be a winner!

Preparation time: 15 minutes
Cooking time: 1¾–2 hours
Serves: 4

1 Soak the bread in the milk for half an hour or overnight.

2 Soak the dried fruit with the lemon or orange juice and brandy overnight.

3 Mix everything together with the margarine, Demerara sugar, mixed spice, egg and nutmeg. Stir hard.

4 Put into a 1-litre (2-pint) greased pie dish. Sprinkle a little sugar on top and decorate with glacé cherries and walnuts, if you like.

5 Cook in a preheated oven, 180°C (350°F), Gas Mark 4 for 1¾–2 hours. Serve while still warm in big hunks.

You Will Need

- 200g (8oz) bread (torn into bits)
- 300ml (½pt) milk
- 175g (6oz) dried fruit
- Good squeeze of lemon or orange juice
- Good slosh of brandy
- 75g (3oz) margarine
- 25g (1oz) Demerara sugar
- 1 tsp mixed spice
- 1 egg
- A little grated nutmeg
- Glacé cherries & walnuts, roughly chopped (optional)

Spicy chicken
Enchiladas

Leftover roast chicken from the weekend is perfect to make these tasty enchiladas.

Preparation time: 20 minutes
Cooking time: 25 minutes
Serves: 6

You Will Need

- 2 tsp veg oil
- 1 large onion, chopped
- 250g (8oz) tin pinto beans
- 300g (10oz) chopped, cooked chicken breast
- 4 green chillies, deseeded & chopped
- 1 tsp dried oregano
- 1 large tomato, chopped
- ¼ tsp chilli powder
- ¼ tsp ground cumin
- 400g (14oz) tin tomatoes
- 12 corn tortillas
- Mango salsa
- 75g (3oz) grated low-fat mozzarella cheese

1 Heat the oil in a saucepan, add the onion and cook for about 5 minutes, until softened. Stir in the beans, chicken, chillies, oregano and fresh tomato. Heat through, then remove from the heat. Place the chilli powder, cumin and tinned tomatoes in a saucepan and simmer for 2 minutes. Remove from the heat.

2 Dip each tortilla into the tomato mixture and set aside. Fill each tortilla with three tablespoons of the chicken mixture. Roll up and place seam-side down in an ovenproof dish. Pour two-thirds of the mango salsa over the enchiladas. Sprinkle with the cheese.

3 Bake in a preheated oven, 180°C (350°F), Gas Mark 4, for about 20 minutes. Place two enchiladas on each plate and serve with the remaining salsa.

ALL IN ONE POT

It will save you time and precious energy to make dishes all in one pot – and there's less washing up too!

Deep-fried tofu &
Stir-fried veg

Boost your five-a-day with this crunchy stir-fry, but make sure veggies retain their bite by being careful not to overcook them.

Preparation time: 10 minutes
Cooking time: 10 minutes
Serves: 4

1 Heat the oil in a wok and fry the garlic for 1 minute. Remove it with a slotted spoon and discard. Add the broccoli, beans and carrots and stir-fry for 3 minutes.

2 Combine the stock, oyster sauce, sugar and chilli sauce in a jug and pour into the wok. Add the tofu and cook for 2–3 minutes, until the tofu is hot and the vegetables are tender. Stir in the bean sprouts and some chopped mint. Serve with boiled white rice.

You Will Need

- 2 tbsp veg oil
- 1 garlic clove, sliced
- 250g (8oz) broccoli florets
- 125g (4oz) green beans, halved
- 2 carrots, thinly sliced
- 150ml (¼pt) hot veg stock
- 3 tbsp oyster sauce
- 2 tbsp brown sugar
- 2 tbsp sweet chilli sauce
- 250g (8oz) cooked tofu
- 125g (4oz) bean sprouts

You Will Need

- 750g (1½lb) lean fillet or leg of lamb
- 1 tbsp plain flour
- 2 tbsp sunflower or veg oil
- 3 onions, cut into wedges
- 400g (14oz) carrots, cut into chunks
- 875g (1¾lb) potatoes, scrubbed & quartered
- 900ml (1½pt) chicken or lamb stock
- 2 bay leaves
- Sprigs of thyme
- 2 tbsp Worcestershire sauce
- Salt & pepper

Warming
Irish stew

Cold weather and dark evenings put us in the mood for traditional, comforting hot food, such as this chunky meat and vegetable stew.

Preparation time: 15 minutes
Cooking time: 1 hour 10 minutes
Serves: 4–5

1 Cut the lamb into even-sized cubes, discarding any excess fat. Season the flour with salt and pepper and coat the lamb.

2 Heat the oil in a large frying pan. Add the lamb and fry for 5–8 minutes until lightly browned. Remove the lamb and transfer to a large flameproof casserole. Add the onions and carrots to the frying pan and fry until lightly browned. Put into the casserole with the potatoes.

3 Add the stock, bay leaves, thyme and Worcestershire sauce to the pan and bring to the boil. Pour into the casserole and season lightly. Cover and cook in a preheated oven, 180°C (350°F), Gas Mark 4, for 1 hour. Check the seasoning.

Creamy spinach &
Haddock chowder

American-style chowders are incredibly easy to make. You just poach the veggies and fish in milk, giving you a creamy, satisfying, calcium-packed soup.

Preparation time: 10 minutes
Cooking time: 25 minutes
Serves: 3

1 Heat the butter and oil in a large saucepan, add the onion and fry gently for 5 minutes, until softened. Add the potato and fry for a further 5 minutes, stirring until lightly browned.

2 Stir in the milk, stock cube, bay leaves, nutmeg and seasoning. Add the haddock, then bring to the boil, cover and simmer for 10 minutes, until the haddock flakes easily. Lift the haddock out, peel off the skin and flake the flesh, removing bones, then set aside.

3 Add the spinach to the pan and cook for 2–3 minutes, until tender. Return the haddock to the pan and reheat. Garnish with the grilled bacon, cut into strips. Serve with crusty bread.

You Will Need

- 25g (1oz) butter
- 1 tbsp sunflower oil
- 1 onion, chopped
- 1 medium baking potato, diced
- 600ml (1pt) semi-skimmed milk
- 1 fish stock cube
- 2 bay leaves
- Freshly grated nutmeg
- 1 smoked haddock fillet, 250g (8oz), halved
- 125g (4oz) young spinach leaves, torn into pieces
- Salt & pepper
- 4 grilled streaky bacon rashers, to garnish
- Crusty bread, to serve

Chicken & spinach
Masala

Chicken and spinach are a great combo and this fragrant Indian recipe uses a variety of delicious spices to enrich the sauce.

Preparation time: 15 minutes
Cooking time: 15 minutes
Serves: 4

1 Heat the oil in a large saucepan. Add the onion, garlic, chilli and ginger. Stir-fry for 2–3 minutes then add the ground coriander and cumin. Stir and cook for 1 minute.

2 Pour in the tomatoes with their juice and cook gently for three minutes. Increase the heat and add the chicken. Cook, stirring, until the outside of the chicken pieces are sealed. Stir in the crème fraîche and spinach.

3 Cover the pan and cook the chicken mixture gently for 6–8 minutes, stirring occasionally. Stir in the chopped coriander with salt and pepper to taste.

- 2 tbsp veg oil
- 1 onion, thinly sliced
- 2 garlic cloves, crushed
- 1 green chilli, deseeded, sliced
- 1 tsp grated fresh ginger
- 1 tsp ground coriander
- 1 tsp ground cumin
- 200g (7oz) tin tomatoes
- 750g (1½lb) chicken thighs, skinned, boned & cut into pieces
- 200ml (7fl oz) crème fraîche
- 300g (10oz) spinach
- 2 tbsp chopped coriander
- Salt & pepper

Moroccan pumpkin &
Lamb cous cous

This exotic combination of lamb with plenty of herbs and spices is a real feast.

Preparation time: 15 minutes
Cooking time: 1 hour 15 minutes
Serves: 4–5

1 Trim any excess fat from the lamb and season. Heat the oil in a large saucepan. Add the onion and fry gently for 3 minutes. Add the lamb and fry until it starts to colour. Stir in the turmeric, chilli powder, cinnamon, ginger, garlic and carrots and fry for 2 minutes.

2 Add the stock and bring to the boil. Reduce the heat, cover with a lid, and simmer on low heat for about 50 minutes until the lamb is tender. Stir in the chickpeas and pumpkin and cook gently for 15 minutes until the pumpkin is tender, adding a little water if the stew looks dry.

3 Meanwhile put the couscous into a bowl and cover with boiling water. Leave, covered, for 5 minutes. Season lightly and fluff with a fork. Stir in the coriander.

You Will Need

- 750g (1½lb) chopped pumpkin
- 425g (14oz) lean lamb
- 75ml (3fl oz) olive oil
- 1 large onion, chopped
- 1 tsp turmeric
- ½ tsp chilli powder
- 1 cinnamon stick
- 2.5cm (1in) piece of fresh ginger, grated
- 3 garlic cloves, sliced
- 2 carrots, sliced
- 600ml (1pt) veg stock
- 410g (14oz) tin chickpeas
- 250g (8oz) couscous
- Handful coriander leaves, chopped
- Salt & pepper

GREEN GRANNY'S PARTY TIME

When you are thinking about throwing a party you might feel that your purse can't take the hit, your efforts to be green will go to the wall, and that you might as well forget the whole idea. But think again. There are plenty of ways of having a hospitable time with friends that are both cheap and green. This section lists some easy entertaining ideas that you can put together pretty quickly – without too many demands on your purse or the planet. Remember: when there are kids around, never leave them unattended near campfires and barbecues.

ALL-AGE PARTIES

Picnic in the park In summer, a great idea is to meet friends in a local park. Everyone brings a dish of food to share. Salads, dips, breads and finger foods are good choices. Arrange who brings what or take pot luck. Take plenty of sacks with you so that no rubbish gets left. Don't forget to separate recyclables.

Summer barbecue Keep the food simple – apart from barbecuing sausages, chicken, steaks and fish provide a selection of salads. Try barbecued bananas for pudding. Wrap bananas (peeled), sprinkle with brown sugar, dust with cinnamon and dot with butter. Seal in foil and grill for eight minutes. A variation is to slit the banana and fill with chocolate chips and marshmallows. This will need about ten minutes. To get your barbecue going:

• Place charcoal in a layer over crumpled paper in the fire basket.
• Pour over a little methylated spirits and light.

- Leave to burn for 20 minutes.
- Rake out the coals and cover with more charcoal. Let it burn for 30 minutes or until you have a steady-burning fire. It is ready when it is ash-grey by daylight and glows red in the dark. It should not be burning fiercely.
- Put the food on a grill.

PARTY IDEAS FOR KIDS

Pirate party Ask all the kids to come dressed up as pirates (home-made costumes if they can). Organize a treasure hunt with appropriate clues. You could make a simple tea of treasure island cake, pretend rum punch grog and chocolate pieces of eight.

Movie party Rent a couple of all-time favourites and serve up delicious home-made popcorn, hot dogs and ice creams.

Make-your-own pizza party Invite a handful of guests to make their own pizzas. Provide everyone with aprons (or old shirts) before you start. Supply all the ingredients for the toppings and the bases and let everyone choose and make their own.

GREEN GRANNY SAYS...

"You don't have to spend a lot of money to have a really good time with your friends and family."

Princess party Raid your local Oxfam shop for pieces of wafty fabric and old curtains. Dress everyone up when they arrive. Serve a 'banquet' of sandwiches, jelly and ice cream.

Campfire party This is a great to try if your theme is 'cowboys and indians'. Set up an improvised 'teepee' at the end of the garden and cook the meal over an open campfire. Enlist the help of other adults to make sure everyone keeps safe near the fire. Cook sausages and hot dogs, toast marshmallows on sticks and heat up some popcorn. Everyone will love getting involved. To make a campfire (an adult should do this):

• Find two logs and put a pile of small, dry sticks between them.
• Light the sticks (kindling), using firelighters and let the fire become established.
• Balance your cooking utensil on the two logs.

PARTY IDEAS FOR GROWNUPS

Cupcake tea party Raid your local charity shops, such as Oxfam, for old-fashioned cups and saucers in which to serve a choice of teas. A mismatched set will add to the occasion's charm. Make some colourful iced cup cakes and some traditional scones to serve with home-made jam (see page 71) and cream.

Brunch party This is a great way to serve a meal for friends in a relaxed way and it's very easy on your purse. Make up some buck's fizz and serve a simple meal of sausage, egg and chips followed by fresh fruit salad. Then toast and marmalade (see page 72) if anyone's got room. If you feel more ambitious you could make pancakes (see page 96).

Cards party Depending on your friends, this could be proper bridge or something more light-hearted. Serve up a casual supper of delicious home-made burgers and chips to eat while you play.

How to make a proper
Cup of tea

Teabags? Forget it! When you're having a proper tea party you need to serve tea the correct way – in style!

1 Boil a kettle of water. Before it has come to the boil pour a little into the tea pot, swirl it around to warm it for a few minutes and pour away.

2 Put about four teaspoonfuls of a loose-leaf tea, depending on how many you are catering for. A good rule of thumb is to allow 1 teaspoonful per 250ml (8fl oz) water.

3 As the water is boiling, pour over the tea leaves and fill the pot. Put on a tea cosy to keep it hot and leave to stand for a few minutes. Refill the kettle and boil it.

4 Pour the tea into the cups. When the pot is half empty refill with boiling water.

5 Some people prefer to put milk in first, some afterwards, while some people don't take milk at all. Offer white sugar and slices of lemon plus teaspoons for stirring. After a while, offer refills.

~ chapter 3 ~

Thrifty fun for everyone

There are so many ways of having fun without spending lots of money. This chapter gives you a few hints and tips on making presents, before exploring ways of having fun for free – out and about or at home. Last, but not least, there are tips on pampering yourself, with a range of easy-to-make beauty products.

MAKE
PERFECT PREZZIES

Presents are important things. They are a symbol of how much everyone cares for each other and come with special 'energy' attached. A present made with the right care and feeling transmits the love of the giver to the receiver. Keep a diary of what you give, to whom, and when, as a reminder for later occasions.

Have you ever though about making presents yourself? How much nicer is it to receive something really original that's been made at home – possibly from recycled materials? If you've got children, they will love making things too. Get them to save suitable bits and pieces – many items can be used to make other things. For example, fabric scraps can be used to make rag dolls (see page 118) and

GREEN GRANNY SAYS...

"Encourage kids to make presents and cards rather than buying them."

Secret Santa

This is a fun idea, because no one knows who is choosing their present for them and it saves so much money! It's a great idea for groups of people – big and small. You just write everyone's names on separate pieces of paper, ahead of time. Each person draws a name out of the hat and buys (or, if possible, makes) a gift for that one person. If you like you can devise a theme – such as 'kitsch'.

You should have a price-limit to stop people spending more than is necessary. Another way to do it is to just put all the presents into a lucky dip – everyone takes pot luck.

if you've got a lot of leftover oranges, they can try making a pretty pomander or a charming christingle (see pages 122–3).

In this section you'll find some easy ideas, which can be made from ordinary bits and pieces you've probably already got, just waiting for a new purpose in life. Also, think about making things people can consume. These days, it's often touch and go whether the recipient will already have what you are about to buy them, or whether they will like the item you have chosen. So consider making things people can eat, such as biscuits, jams and preserves (see pages 71–3) or pamper themselves with (see pages 134–9).

Give a goat!

A great deal of money circulates in the cause of present-buying every year. This may be good for the economy, but think of the energy all these goods need to be manufactured! Why not give the money you would spend to a charity instead – such as Oxfam? Some charities have special 'present-giving' schemes whereby you can support them by giving someone a goat or school equipment, for example. Then you can explain to your friend that the goat is going to someone who needs it more than they need a present.

EVERLASTING PRESENTS

Families often have a 'joke' present that no one is quite brave enough to get rid of. Maybe it's something they received a long time ago (a jester's hat? stripy toe socks? a rubber chicken?). The idea is to wrap the present up every year and give it to an unsuspecting recipient. No one knows who's going to get it and no one wants it, but they have to receive it and then hand it on the next year.

GREEN GRANNY SAYS...

"Don't forget, when you are giving presents – it's the thought that counts."

PRICE-LIMITING

In an age when people can spend a small fortune every year on presents, it's a good plan to agree within your family or group of friends to limit the amount spent on each present. This can be as low as you like. The lower you make it the more inventive people have to be. They can make things, recycle things, or just think in an innovative way. Remember – it's the thought that counts! Don't forget that people will always tend to spend a little more than the limit – so it's good to keep it pegged low.

Wrap it up!

The wrapping paper you buy in the shops has got to be the biggest waste. It's expensive and usually quite high quality – it looks a treat – only to be ripped off in a frenzy, screwed up and thrown into the waste-paper basket – all in a few minutes. A little care could give the paper a new lease of life. Why not try wrapping up your prezzies without using any sticky tape? That way, the recipient can just untie the ribbon and smooth out the paper to use another time. Slightly crumpled paper can be ironed quite safely. If you want to get rid of sellotape, try ironing it off gently. For a 'recycled' look, use newspaper or old magazines as wrapping paper. It can look very effective, particularly when combined with pretty recycled ribbon and home-made gift tags. You can make nice gift bows out of old colourful magazine pages.

THE PRESENT BOX

If you have a few presents that people have given you in the past that you don't want to keep, why not save them in a special 'present box'? You can find the gifts easily for the next birthday or anniversary that comes along. Label them clearly, though, as it would be awkward if you sent them back to the same person!

Avoid doing all your present-shopping at the same time. You'll end up panic-buying and spend more. Try buying presents throughout the year and saving them in a special drawer.

Nice notebooks

This is a great way to recycle that precious resource – paper! It's such a waste to throw away all the computer printouts you've made – you usually won't want to keep most of them. You could make useful notebooks either for yourself or as presents. Make a point of letting people know they're recycled, too!

→ Save up all your computer printouts in a nice neat pile.
→ Using a guillotine, cut them up neatly.
→ Make a cover using some thin card. Either decorate with colourful felt-tipped pens or make a cover out of recycled wrapping paper.
→ Punch a hole in one corner and tie up with some recycled braid or ribbon.
→ Attach a pencil on a pretty ribbon.

How to make a
Button necklace

What could be more unique than a delightful choker made from recycled buttons? If you've got a tin or a jar for collecting them in, have a sort through and pick out some of the more colourful ones. Some charity shops save boxes of buttons so it's worth looking around. Sometimes it's even worth buying charity-shop garments just for the buttons.

1 Thread the buttons in your preferred order – you could consider gradually 'fading' them from dark to light or arranging them in a colour pattern.

2 To add a really stylish touch, you can make a knot in the cord before and after each button.

3 Knot the string after you have decided on your preferred length.

- A square of soft cotton fabric
- Dressmaking scissors
- Wadding, cotton wool or cut-up old tights for stuffing
- Thread or yarn
- Needle & embroidery thread or coloured pens
- Hair-coloured knitting wool (optional)
- Colourful fabric (optional)

How to make a
Comforting doll

Every now and then you may find that you need a present for a baby. If you've got any scraps of plain cotton fabric have a go at making this simple rag doll. It's half way between a doll and a comfort blanket.

1 Cut a square of soft fabric. The size depends on how big you want the finished doll to be. Choose a small size for a baby and a larger one for a toddler.

2 Fold the square in half, diagonally, to form a triangle. Find the centre of the folded edge, bunch up the fabric and stuff it with wadding, cotton wool or cut-up tights to make the doll's head. Pinch in at the 'neck' and wrap round and round securely with thread or yarn.

3 Choose a smooth side for the face and pull any creases to the back of the head. Sew or draw on any features (eyes, mouth, nose). Keep these fairly simple.

4 Sew on hair using recycled knitting wool. Knot the ends of the folded edge to make hands. Add clothes, if you wish.

How to make
Lavender bags

Sweet-smelling lavender bags, made from hankies, make charming presents.

1 Place the hankie on a flat surface and arrange the dried lavender in the centre.

2 Bring the four corners of the hankie together and tie them securely with a piece of ribbon from your scrap store.

GREEN GRANNY SAYS...

"Put lavender bags under your pillow to help you sleep or in your wardrobe to make your clothes smell sweet and to deter moths."

How to make a snake
Draught excluder

Do your socks always seem to lose their partners in the wash? Somewhere, somehow all the lost socks have got together to meet up with new partners – quite a party! The good news is that the ones left behind can be re-used. This project is especially good if you have a collection of stripy socks that need a second life.

1 Choose one sock to be the 'tail' and one to be the 'head'. Cut the tops and bottoms off all the other socks. Sew the sections together. Stuff with cut-up tights or wadding.

2 Sew on two buttons for eyes on the 'head'. Poke in the 'mouth' and sew in a ribbon tongue (cut into a fork for authenticity).

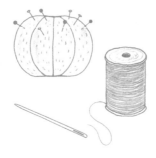

How to make a scented
Candle

Making candles is really easy and loads of fun. They make great prezzies and you can recycle leftover wax from old candles.

1 Heat the wax in a double boiler to 160°C (320°F). You need to watch the temperature to make sure the wax doesn't get too hot. While you are doing this, preheat the candle jar in the oven on the lowest setting.

2 When the wax reaches 160°C (320°F), mix the scented oils and stir in. Then add the food colouring and stir.

3 Take the glass jar out of the oven and carefully pour the wax mixture into the jar. Leave room at the top and save a little wax for topping up. Straighten the wick and lower the metal disk into the melted wax, placing the disk at the centre.

4 Let the candle cool (up to six hours) so that there is a semi-hard crust on top. Adjust the wick so that it is centred. After cooling, the wax will have sunk in the middle so you can reheat the remaining wax and pour in to fill. Allow to cool and trim the wick.

- Double boiler
- Thermometer
- Candle wax (either recycled old candle ends or purchased candle-wax chips)
- Glass container with a lid (for the candle)
- Wick (you can buy this in craft shops)
- Essential oils
- Food colouring

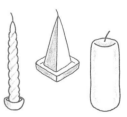

- Spice mixture of
  1 tbsp each of
  ground cinnamon,
  nutmeg and cloves
- 4 drops of
  sandalwood oil
- Toothpick or
  knitting needle
- An orange
- 25g (1oz) large-
  headed cloves
- A paper bag
- Ribbon for
  hanging the
  pomander

How to make a
Pomander

**Pomanders were traditionally used to mask
bad smells around the house, or taken out
by ladies to hold to their delicate noses.
These days you can use them to fill your
home with sweet-smelling freshness as they
are a natural air-freshener and serve as a
moth-repellant too.**

1 Mix the spices with the sandalwood oil in
a bowl and set aside. Using the knitting
needle or toothpick, make holes all over the
orange, pretty close together and poke the
cloves into them.

2 Place the spice mixture in the paper bag
and roll the orange in it until evenly
coated. Leave the orange in the paper bag in a
cool, dry place for four to six weeks to dry out,
rolling it in the spices again every day. When it
is properly dried it will sound hollow when
you tap it. When it is properly dry, remove
from the bag and shake off excess spices.

3 Tie the pomander up with the ribbon.
When the scent starts to fade, add a few
drops of clove oil to your spice mixture and
reroll the pomander in the spices.

How to make a
Christingle

These are an old Christian custom celebrating God's gifts. Kids love to make and hold them and it's a great idea for them to make extras to give to friends and relatives.

1 Cut a small cross in the top of an orange. Cover the cut with a 7cm (3in) square of kitchen foil. Push a candle into the cut.

2 Push dried fruits and nuts onto four cocktail sticks. Insert them into the orange at right angles to each other.

3 Tie recycled wrapping ribbon around the orange and finish it off with a nice bow.

- A decent-sized orange
- Kitchen foil
- A plain candle
- Dried fruits & nuts
- Cocktail sticks
- Reused wrapping ribbon in a contrasting colour (red or green is nice at Christmas time)

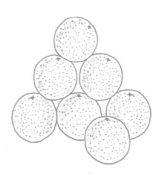

GREEN GRANNY'S FAMILY FUN

We hear a lot about families not spending enough time together and the dire consequences of kids spending too much time in their rooms playing computer games – you've heard it all before! Well, it is much nicer to spend time together as a family, especially if you've got something engrossing to occupy you all – you get to do enjoyable things together, leading to plenty of informal chat and bonding. It's all good! It just takes a bit of thought and effort, but it really is worth it.

If you're into being creative and recycling things, you will be able to find loads of things you can all do together, whether you're at home on a rainy day, out and about, on holiday or just have a free afternoon to amuse yourselves. You'll be amazed how much kids enjoy making things and it's a great way of learning and being creative too. And you'll be able to use up some of your recyclables. If you have 'crafty' friends and family, get together to trade clever ideas for making things – swap your skills.

OUT AND ABOUT

When you're outside it's a good idea to make a special point of either walking or cycling. Exercise, fresh air – sounds corny doesn't it? But it's so very important.

A walk in a park or, better, open countryside, is an adventure in itself. You can let kids go ahead and look for landmarks – older children can be put in charge of a map and asked to find the way. Ordinance survey maps come with a helpful key showing details that kids can look for – the thrill of the chase will get them involved and feel engrossed in what they are doing; far more interesting than just being led along by the grownups.

TRY A NATURE WALK

If you need a stronger focus to keep small ones involved, think about taking a pocket reference book with you and doing a 'tree walk'. You simply walk from one tree to the next and look them up in the book as you go. A great way to learn about the natural world. You can do the same with flowers, birds and animals. Of course, if you're in a city you can do the same thing in parks, or you can look at interesting buildings. Kids can have a special notebook to write down notes about what they've seen and draw pictures. If you have a camera you can take photographs too.

TAKE TO TWO WHEELS

Cycle rides are great, too. The world goes by a little more rapidly, but there's still time to explore and absorb your surroundings. And, of course, this is the time to teach children about the rules of the road so that they can learn how to cycle safely and appropriately.

MAKE A COLLECTION

When you're out, it's a great idea to collect things – provided you're intending to do something with what you collect and you're not removing things that can't be replaced. It's not on to plunder woodlands and beaches with no intention of doing anything with what you gather. Also, be moderate about what you remove. Some places discourage people from taking things away. For example, it may not be acceptable to pick wild flowers – if everyone did it there'd be none left, so it's best to check first. However, with that in mind, it's quite OK to take a few shells from a beach or a few pebbles to make paperweights.

On the beach, have a look for smooth or interestingly shaped pebbles. Perhaps you can find unusually coloured pebbles. Large ones can be turned into doorstops, or used to decorate the garden, while smaller ones can be painted, varnished and turned into paperweights. Very tiny ones can be turned into minimonsters. Just paint on eyes and glue on bent paper clips for legs.

When you're on the beach collect shells. Use it to frame an old mirror – the perfect reminder of your holiday. Driftwood-collecting is a great pastime, too. You can make a wonderful still life in an unused fireplace or on a windowsill.

Gather different-coloured leaves in Autumn – as many different shapes and colours as possible. Press them (see opposite) and use them to make collages and stick them on greetings cards.

How to
Press flowers

Just take a couple of each type of flower – to be sure there are some left for others to enjoy. This is an old-fashioned hobby, but it helps kids (and adults, for that matter) identify and appreciate wild flowers and is well worth doing. You can also press leaves.

You Will Need

- A selection of good flower specimens, freshly picked
- A sheet of newspaper
- A large, heavy book such as an encyclopedia
- More heavy books – about 9kg (20lb) worth

1 After picking your flowers, prevent them from wilting by putting them in the fridge.

2 Place the flowers on the inside fold of a sheet of newspaper. Be careful not to overlap leaves, petals or stems and fold the top half of the newspaper over the flowers.

3 Open the heavy book and place the newspaper in the middle.

4 Close the book and place other books or heavy objects on top. Leave them for about three days.

5 Once the flowers are pressed and completely dry you can arrange them in a presentation album – or however you like.

RAINY DAYS

Rainy days often come as a disappointment, but for families they are a great chance to get down to some of the things that it's hard to find the time for normally. It's worth keeping a list of 'things to do' handy, so that you are never short of good suggestions.

One of the negatives of the 'modern age' is the amount of time children seem to spend in front of a screen – watching TV or playing computer games seem to have become 'default activities' for the majority and a whole raft of stimulating pastimes and activities seem to have been forgotten about. Such a shame! These ideas are usually more or less free, and they're often stimulating, fun, educational, creative, productive and green – you name it! Don't forget, if you're away on holiday, whether in a hotel, guest house, house swap, or camping – always take a good selection of classic board games and a few packs of cards. Hours of fun can be had when the weather's too bad to go out.

GREEN GRANNY
SAYS...

"Why not try guessing what everyone is making with their play dough? It's great fun for all ages."

How to make
Play dough

Play dough is great stuff for young children. They can make little figures, animals, or monsters. If you have food dye in your kitchen cupboard, make several batches so that colours can be mixed and matched.

You Will Need

- 1 cup flour
- 1 cup water
- ½ cup kitchen salt
- 1 tbsp cooking oil
- 1 tbsp cream of tartar
- Drops of vanilla essence
- Food dyes

1 Mix everything, except the food dye, up in a saucepan. Cook over low heat – keep stirring continuously.

2 The mixture will turn into a ball. When this happens, remove from the heat. Leave to cool for a short time and divide into two chunks.

3 When the dough is cool enough to handle, add a few drops of food dye to each ball and knead in. For more than two colours – repeat the process, using other colours.

4 Store in airtight containers such as reused margarine tubs.

You Will Need

- 4 old shoe boxes
- Recycled cardboard
  - cereal packets
    are ideal
- Flour & water
  paste (see step 1)
- Emulsion paint
- Scraps of
  wallpaper,
  fabric, felt,
  old matchboxes,
  thread spools,
  corks, cardboard
  tubes, egg
  cartons, pipe
  cleaners, tissue
  paper

**To make flour &
water paste**
- ½ cup flour
- 3 cups boiling
  water
- 3-4 cups cold
  water

How to make a recycled
Dolls' house

**This is a project all ages can get involved in
and with a little adult supervision, even the
smallest child can take part. Making it will
take plenty of creativity and it will use up
lots of recycled bits and pieces. The end
result will give hours of fun and creative
play. So collect up all those old shoe boxes
and you'll need a good supply of trimmings
and scraps too. The sky's the limit as to how
intricate you want to make the dolls' house.**

1 To make the flour and water paste: slowly
pour cold water into the flour and stir to
make a paste. Pour the paste into the boiling
water, stirring constantly. Cook for five
minutes or until the paste is thick and smooth.
When cool, pour into a plastic container.

2 Paper the 'walls' using scraps of wallpaper
or recycled wrapping paper and the flour
and water paste. Paper the 'floors' with 'carpet'
made from fabric or felt.

3 Cut flaps in the box sides to make 'doors'
and 'windows' (these could have shutters).
Make 'curtains' from fabric scraps, thread on
to elastic thread and staple in place.

4 Make 'beds' (use fabric scraps for bedding) and 'chests of drawers' from recycled matchboxes. Make 'tables' from thread spools and plastic lids and 'chairs' from halved corks or cardboard tubes and egg cartons.

5 Stick the four boxes together, open sides facing out. Create a 'roof' with cereal packets and add a 'chimney' made from a matchbox. Add other touches such as 'fireplaces' (using pictures of fires from old magazines). Make 'lampshades' from old greetings cards.

6 Make little dolls from pipe cleaners and fabric scraps – create a whole family. Paint the outside with 'brickwork' or stick on appropriate recycled wrapping paper to create the effect. Stick on tissue-paper flowers for roses climbing up the walls.

GREEN GRANNY SAYS...

"This is a great creative project that will use up all your old shoe boxes, fabric scraps and cotton reels."

You Will Need

- A long piece of willow
- Strong thread - nylon is good

Decorations

- Fir cones
- Shells with holes in
- Stones with holes in
- Seeds
- Dried leaves
- Dried seaweed
- Dried mosses

How to make a
Mobile

When you are out on walks or on holiday on the beach, collect 'found' objects and make a mobile for a young child. You can hang it over their cot, or in a place which catches air currents. Choose objects to reflect the season. If the mobile is to be hung over a cot, be sure to choose items that do not drop seeds or fall to pieces easily – these could be a choking hazard. If in doubt hang the mobile away from the cot.

1 Bend the strip of willow into a ring, twisting it around itself. Tie it firmly at regular intervals.

2 Cut three threads and tie centrally at the top to hang the mobile from. Cut different-length threads and tie the decorations to them. You can tie several objects from the same thread if you like.

3 Tie the decorated threads to the willow ring. You will need to make sure the balance is even. Hang the mobile somewhere where the baby or child can see it, but where he/she can't actually grab it.

How to make a
Toy theatre

You Will Need

- 2 same-sized cardboard boxes
- Paints for decorating the theatre
- Lengths of garden dowelling
- Glue
- Old magazines for cutting out characters

Theatres provide children with hours of creative play – and you get to use up plenty of recycled bits during the making of it. Encourage kids to invent their own plays and characters and give a performance at the next family event.

1 Cut an arch in the front of one of the boxes. Paint the whole box, inside and out, in the colours of your choice. Cut a matching pair of slots in the top of each side of the box to hold the scenery. Make scenery from the other box and suspend it from the dowelling rods. Cut openings in each side of the theatre to slide the characters in and out.

2 Cut characters from old magazines, stick them on recycled card and stick them onto folded strips to operate from the 'wings'.

3 You could also manipulate characters from the top of the theatre – attach a piece of dowelling to the head from the top instead. Make a stage curtain from scraps and thread it onto elastic. Staple it in place.

TREAT YOURSELF: PAMPERING

Well, when you've finally reached the last part of this book, you'll be in need of a good rest and perhaps a little natural pampering. Why not treat yourself and your friends?

A whole industry has developed based on grooming and pampering. Although hairdressers have been a feature of the high street for a very long time, it's amazing to think that nail bars are relatively recent developments –

unheard of not so many years ago! It's perfectly possible to do your nails yourself, plus many of the other beauty treatments available.

On top of this, you'll have noticed that another whole industry is based around the lotions and potions needed to pamper ourselves with and it would be perfectly possible to spend a small fortune without even noticing. However, with a little time and patience it's easy to make many of these items yourself, using ingredients you probably already have. Some of these home-made lotions and potions will come out so well that you may even want to turn them into presents for friends and relatives.

It would be great to have a weekly pampering session – a fun way to wind down and relax after a hard week. Well, why not create your own special time for this at home? Maybe you could hold your own 'pamper parties' and invite friends. More fun that way and you can share ideas about making your own lotions and potions.

MAKE A HOME SPA

If you just need some 'me-time' there's plenty you can do to create your own spa at home without spending money. Just work with what you already have. Allow 20-30 minutes.

🖐 Clear the bathroom of other people's stuff, particularly kids' toys and any other distractions.

🖐 Search out a couple of your nicest towels – the fluffier the better. You'll need one big one for your body and a smaller one to swathe your head in. Washcloths will come in handy too. Gather up your bathrobe and slippers.

🖐 Put some relaxing music on and light some scented candles to arrange around the bath (see page 121 if you want to make your own). Lavender is great if you want to relax and citrus is good for rejuvenation.

🖐 Get your home spa treatments ready in a convenient place – a little basket would be perfect.

🖐 Run your bath and add, for example, lavender oil to the water for deep relaxation. A lovely rich mud mask will moisturize and soothe. If you need to energize yourself try out peppermint oil in your bath water and have a cucumber mask.

🖐 Turn off the main lights, light the candles and turn on your music. Wash your face with a warm facecloth and put on your facial mask.

🖐 Apply an exfoliating scrub and relax completely in your bath.

🖐 Rinse off and wrap yourself up in your towels. Maybe it's time for a delicious jasmine or chamomile tea.

SPA ACCOMPANIMENTS

There are a myriad different things you can try out during your spa session. Everyone is different, so these are a few suggestions to try – see what works best for you. Don't be afraid to experiment. Be sure to test a small area of your skin or hair first to ensure that home-made products do not cause an adverse reaction.

Herbal bath
Teas

Try making teas to put in your spa bath water; they are easy to make and use. Use small muslin bags (sew your own with a muslin scrap and tie it tightly at the top with ribbon).

1 Add about half a cup of each herb to your muslin bag and steep in a basin of boiling water for about 10–15 minutes.

2 Run your bath and pour the bath tea into it. Swirl it around to mix it in.

3 Tie your muslin bag to the taps as well and allow it to soak in your bath.

Herbal hair
Conditioner

Give your hair a regular refresher by trying this all-purpose conditioner

1 Place the herbs in the top of a double boiler and add the oil. Heat for 30 minutes. Pour into a wide-mouthed jar. Cover with a piece of muslin secured with a ribbon. Stand this in a warm place for about a week, stirring every day. Then strain the oil into a clean jar.

2 To use, warm about half a cup of the oil, less if your hair is shorter, over very low heat for a few minutes.

3 Rinse your hair with hot water and squeeze out excess water.

4 Rub the warm oil into your hair and scalp. Cover with a shower cap, then a warm, damp towel.

5 Condition for 20–30 minutes, then shampoo to remove the oil.

You Will Need

- ½ cup dried chamomile flowers
- ¼ cup dried rosemary leaves
- 1 cup safflower or sunflower oil
- Wide-mouthed jar
- Piece of muslin and a length of ribbon.

For cream facial
- 1 tsp honey
- 2 tbsp whipping cream

For lemon facial
- ½ tsp lemon juice
- 2 tbsp honey

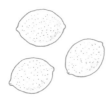

Honey
Facials

Honey is a great tonic for the face. These two facials are easy to make and even easier to apply and use. Always patch-test a small area of skin and wait 24 hours before applying new products to your face – if irritation occurs discontinue use.

Honey & cream facial

1 Combine one teaspoon honey with two tablespoons of heavy whipping cream.

2 Beat together and, when it reaches the right consistency, pat onto your face, rubbing gently and smoothing your skin.

3 Leave on for a few minutes, then rinse with warm water.

Honey & lemon facial

1 Combine half a teaspoon of lemon juice with two tablespoons of honey. Blend together and spread over your entire face.

2 Leave on for 15–20 minutes, then rinse with warm water and gently pat dry with a soft towel.

DIY
Manicure

Try this DIY manicure at home – it's a relaxing, natural way of giving your nails a treat. Try it on your friends too.

1 Take off any nail varnish you are already wearing, using nail-varnish remover.

2 Soften your hands and nails in a bowl of warm water for about ten minutes.

3 Use a cotton bud to remove any dirt from beneath the nails.

4 Ease back your cuticles with a cotton bud dipped into the rosehip oil.

5 File your nails with the emery board, working from the outside inwards.

6 Use a little avocado or rosehip oil to massage into your hands.

You Will Need

- Nail varnish remover
- Large bowl of warm water
- Cotton buds
- Rosehip oil
- Soft emery board
- Avocado oil

QUICK BEAUTY FIXES

There are loads of quick and easy beauty tips you can try at home. Here is a short selection to try out:

To remove nail yellowness Just dip the tips in lemon juice for ten minutes.

Make your own mouthwash Dissolve two tablespoons of apple cider vinegar and one teaspoon of salt in a glass of warm water. You can now approach your friends after you've eaten garlic or onions.

For tooth whitening Brush with bicarbonate of soda.

For tired eyes Lie down in a quiet, dark room and rest with cold teabags or cold cucumber slices over your eyes.

Soothe a cold sore Put a little distilled vinegar on a cotton ball and dab it on your cold sore three times a day. You'll find that it helps reduce pain and swelling.

Exfoliate Add a little sugar to some ordinary baby oil and rub it thoroughly into your face. Wash off after a few minutes have elapsed.

Green Granny's pampering tip

Why not try getting your friends together to have a Pampering Party? Everyone can take turns blow-drying each other's hair, doing facials and trying out makeup on each other. If you want to be really brave you can have a go at cutting each other's hair. Look online for instructions or buy a DVD on how to cut hair. You will save loads of money and have fun at the same time.

Skin solutions

ACNE First wash your face as usual and then dab your skin with a mixture of one part apple cider vinegar and ten parts water. This will help balance the PH in your skin.

SUNBURN Soak a soft towel in an equal-part mixture of apple cider vinegar and water and apply to the area for as long as possible.

TONING Make up a finishing rinse by mixing one tablespoon of apple cider vinegar with two cups of warm water. Put it on your face and leave it to dry.

MAKEUP REMOVER If you've run out of makeup remover and cleanser try using cold milk instead.

Hair solutions

MORE BODY If you need to add more body to your hair try rinsing it in beer after shampooing. Rinse off thoroughly afterwards.

HAIR CONDITIONER A quick, cheap conditioner can be made from egg yolk, which you should rinse off in cold water. No need to go for an expensive hot-oil conditioning treatment when you can just massage in olive oil. Make sure you rinse it off afterwards.

EASY HERBAL HAIR RINSE Pour two cups of boiling water over two tablespoons of dried rosemary. Steep this for 15 minutes, strain and rinse hair with the water to give your hair a nice shine.

IMPROVE HAIR GROWTH Use your ordinary shampoo, but add one drop each of rosemary and lavendar essential oil to one tablespoon of your normal shampoo.

INDEX

Bold page numbers
indicate recipes &
'How to' instructions.

A

acne 141
allotments 64
altering clothes 40
ammonia 25
apples, recipes **73**, **97**

B

baby food 68
bag for life **52**
bags, shopping 50, 51, **52**, 53
bananas 68, **96**, 106
barbecues 106–7
bath teas **136**
bathrooms 16–17, 135
beans, recipes **75**, **79**
beauty care 134–41, **136–9**
bedding 19, 22–3, 26
bicarbonate of soda 13, 14,
    15, 16, 17, 19, 21, 26, 27,
    35, 70, 140
bleach 14, 15, 16
blinds 24
blocked sinks 15
book swaps 53
box schemes 60
bread-based recipes **75**, **82**,
    98, **99**
buttons **37**, 41, **117**

C

cages 27
candles **121**, **123**, 135
capsule wardrobe 32
carpets 22, 25–6, 27
cat litter trays 27

cauliflower crumble **81**
charity gift schemes 114
charity shops 29, 33, 40, 41,
    54–5, 108
cheese, recipes **76**, **80**, **87**
chicken, recipes **90–1**, **100**,
    104
chickpeas, recipes **77**, **105**
children
    baby food 68
    clothes 34, 40
    entertaining 107–8,
        124–6, **127**, 128, **129–33**
    toys 41, 53, **118**, **129–33**
chilli bean soup **79**
chocolate bread & butter
    pudding **98**
chowder **103**
christingles **123**
chutney, apple **73**
cleaning 10, 12–27, 69
clothes 32–3
    capsule wardrobe 32
    children 34, 40
    defluffing 20
    laundry 18–21
    mending 11, 36, **37–9**, 40
    moth prevention 22–3,
        119
    personalizing 40–1
    recycling 33–4, 41, 50,
        53, **56–7**, **120**
    shoes 35
    warmth 49
clutter corners 28
cola 16
cold sores 140
collars, stained 19
collecting 126, **132**
conditioner, hair **137**, 141

cooking *see* food &
    cooking
couscous **105**
credit cards 46–7
curtains 24
cushion covers 40
customizing clothes 41
cycle rides 125

D

darning **38–9**
decluttering 28–31, 49
decorating 42, 44–5
defluffing jumpers 20
detergents 17, 18
diaries, spending 48
dishwashers 14
DIY 10, 42–5
dolls **118**
dolls' houses **130–1**
draught excluders 41, **120**
dressing-up parties 107,
    108
driers 19–20
driftwood 126
dry-cleaning 20
dust mites 19, 23
dusting 25
duvets 19, 22, 23
dyeing 41

E

eggs 67, **87**, **89**, 141
embroidery 41
enchiladas **100**
exfoliating 135, 140
eyes, tired 140

F

facials, honey **138**

falafel cakes **77**
family fun 124–8, **127–33**
first aid kit 11
fish 61, **83**, **88–9**, **92–3**, **103**
floors 15, 22, 25–6, 27
flowers 65, 126, **127**
food & cooking
  grow your own 62, **63**, 64
  parties 106–8, **109**
  recipes **70**, **71–3**, **75–105**
  shopping 47, 60–1, 71
  storage 67–9
  tips 50, 66–8, **70**, 74
  wild foods 65
foraging 65
fridges & freezers 15,
  68–9
frittatas **87**
fruit 60, 61, 65, 66–68,
  71, 74
  recipes **71–3**, **96–7**
furniture 42
fuses, changing **43**

G
gammon, glazed **86**
gardening 11, 17, 53, 62,
  63, 64
glass, cleaning 24
goat-giving 114
grass stains 19
grooming pets 27
grouting, cleaning 14

H
haddock chowder **103**
hair care **137**, 141
ham, recipes **86**, **87**
hammers 45
heating bills 49
herbs 62, 68, **119**, **136–7**,
  141
hobs, cleaning 13
home spas 134–41, **136–9**
honey facials **138**

I, J
Irish stew **102**
ironing 20, 21
jam, strawberry **71**
jambalaya **91**
jumpers
  care & repair 20, 21,
    38–9
  recycling 41, 50, **57**

K
kedgeree **89**
kettles 13
kitchens 13–15, 69
kits 10–11

L
lamb, recipes **102**, **105**
lasagne **80**, **85**
laundry 18–21
lavender **119**, 135, 136
leather care 35
leaves 126, **132**
leftovers 68
lemon juice 10, 14, 15, 68,
  138, 140
lightbulbs, changing **43**
limescale 13, 14, 15, 16, 18,
  21
litter trays 27
loos, cleaning 16

M
macaroni cheese **76**
mackerel, recipes **88–9**
makeup removal 141
manicures **139**, 140
marmalade, Seville **72**
masala **104**
maybe sacks 31
meat 61, **84–7**, **90–1**, **100**,
  102, **104–5**
memory quilts **56–7**
mending 11, 36, **37–9**, 40
microwave cooking 67

mince-meat sauce **85**
money 46–9, 113, 115, 116
Moroccan couscous **105**
moths 22–3, 119
mould 16
mouthwashes 140
mushroom lasagne **80**

N
nail care **139**, 140
nature walks 125–6
necklaces, button **117**
notebooks **116**

O
oranges **72**, **122**, **123**
outdoor activities 106–7,
  108, 125–6
oven cleaning 13

P, Q
packaging 50, 51, **52**, 53,
  115
painting 42, 44–5
pampering 134–145, **136–9**
pancakes **96**
panzanella **82**
paper 30, 115, **116**
parties 34, 53, 106–8, **109**,
  140
pasta, recipes **76**, **78**, **80**,
  85, **93**
patches & patchwork **39**,
  56–7
pebbles 126, **132**
peppers, recipes **82**, **91**
pets 27
picnics 106
pillows 23
plants 11, 17, 53, 62, **63**, 64
play dough **129**
plug fuses, changing **43**
pomanders **122**
pork, spiced **84**
pot roast, chicken **90**

potatoes 69, **70**, **83**
presents 112–16, **117–23**, 126
preserves **71–3**
pressing flowers **127**
puddings, recipes **96–9**, 106
pumpkin, recipe **105**

quilts & throws **56–7**

R

radiators, cleaning 25
rag dolls **118**
rainwater 17
rainy days 128, **129–33**
recycling 50–1, 54, 124
  charity shops 29, 33, 40, 41, 54–5, 108
  clothes 33–4, 41, 53, **56–7**, **120**
  decluttering 29
  DIY waste 42
  paper 30, 115, **116**
  swap parties 34, 53
  toys 41, 53, **118**, **130–3**
  unwanted gifts 116
repairs *see* DIY; mending
rice, recipes **70**, **89**, **91**
roasts, recipes **70**, **90**, **92**, **94–5**

S

salmon, recipes **92–3**
saucepans 50
saving money 46–9, 113, 115, 116
saws 44
scented candles **121**
Secret Santa 113
seeds, sprouting **63**
Seville marmalade **72**
sewing 11
  bag for life **52**
  clothes 36, **37–9**, 40, 40–1
  quilts & throws **56–7**
shells 126, **132**

shoe care 35
shoes-off policy 12
shopping 31, 33
  bags 50, 51, **52**, 53
  charity shops 29, 33–4, 40, 41, 54–5, 108
  food shopping 47, 60–1, 71
  money management 46–9, 113, 115, 116
showers 16
sinks 15
skin care **138**, 141
slow cookers 66
smells 15, 18, 24, 25–6, 27, 35, 70
snake draught excluder **120**
soda crystals 16
  see also bicarbonate
soups, recipes **79**, **95**, **103**
spa treatments 134–41, **136–9**
spending diaries 48
spinach, recipes **80**, **103**, **104**
spring cleaning 26
sprouting seeds **63**
stain removal 18, 25, 35
steaming food 66
stir–fry **101**
storing food 67–69
strawberry jam **71**
sunburn 141
sweaters *see* jumpers
sweet potatoes, recipe **88**
swishing parties 34, 53

T

tea 108, **109**, 140
temperature, laundry 18–19
theatres **133**
throws & quilts **56–7**
tiles, cleaning 14
toffee apple bake **97**

tofu, deep-fried **101**
tog ratings 22
toilets *see* loos, cleaning
tomatoes 61, **75**, **78**, **79**, **82**, **85**, **91**, **92**, **100**, **104**
toning skin 141
tools 10, 11, 42, 44, 45
toothbrushes, cleaning with 14, 15, 19
tooth-cleaning 17, 140
  pets 27
toothpaste, stain removal 19, 21
toys 41, 53, **118**, **129–33**
tumble driers 19–20
tuna fishcakes **83**

U, V

underarm stains 19

vacuuming 22, 23, 25, 26
vegetables 60, 61, 64, 66–8, 74
  recipes **70**, **75**, **77**, **80–3**, **88**, **94–5**, **101**
Venetian blinds 24
vinegar
  apple chutney **73**
  beauty care 140, 141
  cleaning agent 10, 15, 18, 19, 24, 25, 26, 27, 35, 69
  descaling agent 13, 14, 16, 17, 18, 21

W

walks 125–6
washing machines 18–19
washing powders 17, 18
washing-up liquid 13, 14, 15, 19, 24
water-saving 16, 17, 50
wild foods 65
window-cleaning 24
worktops, cleaning 14
wrapping paper 115